IN YOU THE AMOZULA

Poems by:

Sarita Gaye Cardwell

Copyright © 2022 **MERIDIAN PRESS**

All rights reserved. No part of this publication may be reproduced distributed, or transmitted in any form or by any means, including photocopying, recording, or other electronic or mechanical method without the prior written permission of the publisher, except in the c of brief quotations embodied in critical reviews and certain other noncommercial uses permitted by copyright law. For permission requests, write to the publisher, addressed "Attention: Book Rights a Permission," at the address below.

Published in the United States of America

ISBN 978-1-958518-05-2 (HC)
ISBN 978-1-958518-06-9 (Ebook)

MERIDIAN PRESS
222 West 6th Street
Suite 400, San Pedro, CA, 90731
www.stellarliterary.com

Order Information and Rights Permission:

Quantity sales. Special discounts might be available on quantity purchases by corporations, associations, and others. For details, cont the publisher at the address above.

For Book Rights Adaptation and other Rights Permission. Call us at to free 1-888-945-8513 or send us an email at admin@stellarliterary.cc

CONTENTS

ACT 1

THROWBACK 4

LEGEND 7

R 11

Y DORPHY 14

RICA 18

GRY KIDS 22

OP HUSTLE 27

MON KILLER 30

GE 33

MOWER NOISE 36

.... 39

T TURNED SKEEZER 42

NG MACHINE 44

.... 47

LOVE 49

E 51

BRAND NEW 53

MBOAT 54

OM 56

CATS 57

BLAZERS 59

BARONESS LIZZY 61

TTING MY STUFF 63

DREAM 65

SEAM 67

- THE CREED
- PIPE DREAMS
- PERSON
- THE WORLD
- ONE ACE
- MAN HANDS
- MAKE YOU WISH THAT YOU WAS
- OLD MAN RIVER
- THE TREE
- MT. KILIMANJARO
- LIZZY'S BOREDOM II
- LISTEN!
- KINKS
- THE DEED
- LET US BE
- AFRANE LUMINOUS
- AMOZEKE! AMAZON! AMO-AFRICANS!
- AIN'T MISBEHAVING
- AFRICA
- THE POWER
- DREAM, DREAM, FREEDOM's BELL
- DREAM
- EARL
- FACING THE HONEST TRUTH LIKE RUTH
- LONG GONE
- I MUST LEAD
- HAVE-NOT LESS-GOT
- HOPE

E IN A WORLD	126
A LITTLE HEAVEN ON EARTH DRUG	127
HT EYES	130
Y	131
RL CALLED STUPID	132
TALK	134
ER THAN THE RIVER	135
AMS AND DESIRES	137
ESCAPADE	138
REAL	141
E	143
AD LOVE	146
ATNESS FOUND	152
BLOOD	155
ECT FIT	157
N ROAD	158
RACE	159
ATIN	161
CATED	162
WINNING HAND	163
VIRGINS	164
R-VIPER PASTURES	165
N BORN	166
HER PLANE	167
R MIND	169
YOUNG	171
KES AND THE LEGEND	173
LOVERS	174

WANTED	1
BETTER DAYS	1
THE JOY	1
A FINER LINE	1
A FINER LINE part 2	1
GIVE IT A REST	1
DOWNHILL	1
THE RAREST FOLK	1
THE ANSWER	1
THE HIGH AND THE MIGHTY	1
THE ENDS THE MEANS	1
THE GOOD SONG	1
MEET AND GREET	1
IT'S CLEAR	20
SOMEBODY'S SWEET FOOL	20
A RARE THING	20
I AM HERE	20
FALSEHOODS	20
THE AGONY THE EBONY	20
THE EXPLOITATION	21
KEEPERS OF THE LEGEND	21
DEADLY STORM	21
DIVIDED UNDECIDED	22
IT'S HEREDITARY	22
AMOZEKE! AMAZON! AMOZULA!	23
AMOZEKE AMAZON AMOZULA PART 2	23
MADE ONE	23
AMOZEKE AMAZON AMOZULA PART 3	23

OZEKE AMAZON AMOZULA PART 4 239

LEGACY OF THE SULTAN 243

AZE AND AMAZON 245

SENSATION OF AMAZE AND AMAZON 246

OZEKE AMAZON LONG GONE 249

ALITIES OF THE Z-KINGS 252

REVELATION OF GREATNESS 253

G OF THE Z-KINGS 255

THE PACT

I was born in wealth
grew up in shame
folks around the way
remembered my name...
Born near the falls
Blessed to walk the
hallowed halls...

Born, born,
I made a pact-
Born, born,
devil get back!

I was born in wealth
grew up in shame
starvation had my
number
poverty knew my name!
Swore to the very end
As many hearts broken
I would mend!

Born, born,
betcha bite a chip...
Born, Born,
Child give me no lip!

I was born, raised...
went to school...

I was praised...
When other folks wasn't...
I had a good name
Whether it gets done or doesn't-
Worked hard through
the pain...

But I made the grade...
Wish I could get paid...
Silence was golden...
Pressure was the pain!

Born, born,
I made a pact...
Born, born,
devil get back!

I was born in wealth,
grew up in shame...
starvation had my number,
and poverty knew my name!
I had a good name...
went from trouble to
fame...

Fame and fortune,
Fortune and fame...
Which comes first
the baby or the name?
The name game
The same rain

Washing over my head...
So cold, I felt like
I was dead!

The same old system
Bless 'em, confess 'em
Miss 'em, and diss 'em!

Born, born,
I made a pact...
Born, born,
devil get back!

Which would you
hold on to?
Which would you
throw away?
Taking it all for
granted....
Wishing that you
could only stay...

Born, born,
I made a pact...
Born, born,
devil get back!

THE THROWBACK

It could be one of those
good things that keep
you warm

But afraid that if I
blink I miss it,
and it be gone!

Come back, throw back,
That mellow curve...
Come back, Lo-jack,
So much action
To singe the raw nerve!

And hands of steel
Hands of feeling
Deep down in your heart
And you know he's for- realing
Without knowing where to start,

COME BACK-
THROW BACK- that mellow curve...

COME BACK-
TO LO-JACK
AND GET READY FOR THE WORLD!

Mellow curve,
Mellow curve...

All the JOY WATISSIMO'S
IN THE WORLD!

Sing you a song...
String you along....
Sing it when I'm long-Gone!
Throwback that mellow curve
With a brassy, sassy, song!

Hear me now and
hear me well...
Life's sweet golden moments
Are the sounds of freedom bells

Ring-Ring,
Sing-sing,
Sing wrong,
Ring wrong!

Go back,
Throw back,
Come back
To LO-Jack!

GO back
Throw back
Come back
TO LO-JACK!

Throwback, go back in time...
Go back, to the place that
started the rhyme!

Go back to the place that
started the blues...

There's just going to be a problem
IF YOU SNOOZE!
Use the time wisely
Live a little, learn a little,
Because life's full of Surprises!

Give a little... Live a little...
One step at a time...

En Amour Amozeke you, to keep you,
so that you can Amo-Arrive!

THE LEGEND

There once was a girl named Dee...And if you laughed your crooked laugh, and showed your crooked smile... She begun to walk a country ole' mile. laughing as she went out the door (where she always stood)... each person would watch her laugh herself a country ole' mile! which to her was good...

with her good friend noname (who remains a mystery)
Like an apple a day keeps the doctor away...

here's the good one that got away... walk with me three miles a day...And we'll see you at the party,
Or legend club...
That's just like your average house or pub!

It's extraordinary
With her all-knowing
look
Said: You're talking
too much death, you
old crook!

The legend never dies
The legend down-to-earth!
Because the legend
never dies...take some
chances for what it's
worth!

If you talks a crooked
talk...and you walks a
crooked walk...and you
smiles a crooked smile...
Walk to the legendary
legends club...where it's
just like your average
house or pub.

And all you heard was
laughter...you couldn't
run or go faster! You had
to stay and outsmart the
master of all masters...
If you can't catch up-just
run faster!

Smoke flowed out of the
mouth and out of the
windows...smoke flowed

through the air...
This is why the legend won't
stop or die in months...
But don't let it catch your
hair!

Because if you has a
crooked laugh, smoke
comes out of your mouth...
You'd get on your horse and
clippedy-clop,
down a country old mile!

The laughter, the legend,
the label won't fade away
or die...
The laughter, the legend,
the label-and you smokes
your smokes and you smiles
your crooked smile...

Because the legend is rumored
to be a place of great evils...
Dee and her friend No-Name
were really great deceivers!
So much smoke that it travels
through the room... but don't
let it catch your hair...

So to ask your when's and
to ask your why's...the laughter,
the legend, the label never fades
away or dies...
So to ask you when's and why's...
I say the legend never closes

or dies...

Who wants to live the legend?
Who's gonna steal the show?
Who wants to live the legend-
because you think you're gonna know!

The laughter, the legend, the label
won't fade away or die...
Smoke goes through the room...
And you ran a good, country ole' mile!

Because it travels through
the room and into the air...
It travels on and on, but don't
let it catch your hair!

Who wants to live the
legend? Who wants to let
it die?
Who wants to live the legend?
And you told your crooked lies!

Though into you, and beyond
the old mirror...
What lives on is what's out there...

Though into you, and beyond
the old mirror...
What lives on is what's out there!

SUPER

Superman, Super bitch!
What you gonna do?
I say what you gonna do
When those walls
All fall down on you?!

I say what you gonna do
When those walls all
Fall down on you!

Jump when they ask
How high ?
Or wait it out like
A prince in a high
Tower?
Is a bull - Or a bully,
Is a bully
To the bitch!
Is a bird?
Is a plane!
Is super bitch!
Once treating for tricks
Got more tricks than sticks,
Super what you want,
Super is what you get!
On your plate or in
Your face!
Jupiter and Kansas have met!
Is super what you want?

Super is what you get!

On your plate,
Or in your face,

Gonna get on your case!!!
Just in time,
This is the place,
Or, should I throw it
in your face?
Hair styled and dressed
To match!
Beauty and the beast
Got love to catch!

Hair styled and dressed
to match...beauty and the
Beast got love to catch!

Beauty in the deep,
Beauty in the west-

Beauty and the beast
Got love to confess!
Confess it, confess it,
Confess it to wit...
Super is what you want
Super is what you get!
I say what you gonna do
when it all falls on you?

Beast and the beauty,
Beauty and the beast,
This is what I'm saying:
Three to the East!

Super is what
You want- Super is what
you get...
Beauty and the beast
got love to get!
Beauty and the beast
Beast and the beauty-
Stomping my feet...
Shaking my booty!
Sha--booty!
The Beauty!
Beast in the deep,
Beauty in the west...
Beauty and the beast
Got love to 'fess!

ORPHY DORPHY

Orphy-Dorphy is what she's called,
She makes such a mess,
And then she's gone,
Just like a pest!

Orphy-Dorphy is what she's called,
Brain like a bubble,
Jezebels mirror image,
Or should I call her Jezze bubble?

Orphy-Dorphy is what she's called,
She sleeps in the nude,
You can't ever be too careful,
Her ass is just plain rude!

Orphy-Dorphy is what she's called,
And this I must confess:
She ain't nothin but trouble,
And just a snotty old pest!

Orphy-Dorphy is what she's called,
Boys trying to have something to see,
When they come to look at Orphy,
They come from as far as Riley street,

Orphy-Dorphy,
Orphy-Dorphy...

Lizzy-Kizzy-Boredom...

    Orphy-Dorphy,
    Orphy-Dorphy,

Leave and take
Some more of them...

    Orphy-Dorphy,
    Orphy-Dorphy,

Lizzy-Kizzy-Boredom...

    Orphy-Dorphy,
    Orphy-Dorphy,

Leave and take
Some more of them...

    Orphy-Dorphy,
    Orphy-Dorphy,

Brain like a bubble...

    Orphy-Dorphy,
    Orphy-Dorphy,

You're asken' for trouble...

    Orphy-Dorphy,
    Orphy-Dorphy,

Brain like a bubble...

    Orphy-Dorphy,
    Orphy-Dorphy,

You're asken' for trouble!

    Orphy-Dorphy,
    Orphy-Dorphy,

Start using your head...

    Orphy-Dorphy,
    Orphy-Dorphy,

You just been misled...

Jezebel-Jezzebubble,
Stop looking for trouble...

    Jezebel-Jezzebubble...
    I'm not your double!

    Jezebel-Jezzebubble...
    Just make a choice...

    Jezebel-Jezzebubble...
    Why can't you rejoice?

Search deep in your heart
And get you some pride...

Search deep in your heart...
Get a brand new start!

    Orphy-Dorphy,
    Orphy-Dorphy,

Lizzy-Kizzy-Boredom...

Orphy-Dorphy,
Orphy-Dorphy,

Leave and take
some more of 'em...

Orphy-Dorphy,
Orphy-Dorphy,

Lizzy-Kizzy-Boredom...

Orphy-Dorphy,
Orphy-Dorphy,

Leave and take
Some more of 'em!

IN AFRICA

In Africa-
Where the saga
begins-

the Amozekes
will detect
when the tides
will come in
Where all the
people had ruled,
and they all was kin!

It's often hard to
detect when the
tides do come in!

I wonder who?
Boy is it you?

Sweat in the sun...
-you don't have have fun!

A risk and a chance
to charm will
enhance our stories
of old that
are bold
tragics told!

A risk and a chance

to charm
will enhance
Our stories of old
that are bold tragics told!

In Africa where the
saga begins

the Amozekes will
detect where the
tides do begin

where all the people
had ruled

and they all was kin!

its often hard to accept
when the tides do begin!

Amozekes, Amazons all over the nation
Amozulas, Amo-Khans to strengthen
The nation!

The old, bold, stories told!
Tragics lost, treasures gained, stories of old
Amozekes, Amazons and legends
unfold!
Amozekes, Amazons, and
the story was told!

Come fly with me!
To our destiny!
And together
we'll see! what

conclusions will be!

In Africa...
Where the world begins...

The outer seas
will
collect
What the tides
do bring in...

From where the people
had ruled
And
They all was kin
It's often hard
To predict where the
tides do begin!

I wonder who?
boy is it you?

Sweat in the sun...
You don't have fun!

A risk and a chance
will serve to enhance
Our stories of old
That are bold tragics
told!

A risk and a chance
will sever to enhance
Our stories of old
That are bold

Tragics told!

In my lions den
There's trouble
and sin...
Don't beat the
drums so slow-
Beat them fast
Then I'll Know!

In my lions den
There's trouble
and sin...
Don't beat the
drums so slow-
Beat them fast!
Then I'll know!

So many people!
So many rulers!
Not many sorrows...

Don't break the rules

A risk and a chance
will serve to enhance
Our stories of old
That are bold tragics
Told!

A risk and a chance
will serve to enhance
Our stories of old
That are bold tragics
told!

HUNGRY KIDS

What's this I see...some faces
Pressed against my window pane?
Whose hungry kids are those...
And why'd they come back again?

Because they get all hungry
For the grub I got...
They act like I'm the only
One in the world...
Should they get what I got?

I wish I could wish 'em up something....
Something they ain't got...
Something to make them go away,
So their stomachs can be in a knot!

In the winter It gets cold,
Have to shovel the snow...
Just where did these hungry kids come from?
That...I just don't know...

But I work hard
For the grub I got...
But who the heck are these hungry kids?
Because their mother...I just am not!

I could pull down my shade
But their shadows still show...
I could toss 'em a bread loaf

But they'd come back for more...

Their mouths say "open the door"
But I won't let them in...
Their minds say grab the grub
These thieves are committing a sin!

Who made these monsters?
Somehow...I'll make 'em go!
Who showed 'em my house?
Now that...I just don't know...

God forgive me if it's witchcraft
I'm willing to admit...
But if I can't stop it
I'd be willing to try and quit!

If they can't help it
I'll pray and ask God to guide their feet home...
And make this their last dance...
And just leave me alone!

Let their thieving thoughts crumble
Turn to ashes and dust...
Let them scatter in the wind...
And stop watching my house!

Let their thieving thoughts never rise
To eyeball my grub...
Turn their sunny skies gray....
My house ain't no pub!

Let them never to imagine...
How they can take my grub...
Let God drop 'em down a big bread loaf...

From the heavens above!

For they want my attention
To ask for my grub...
But their big old eyes just stare...
I wish for the heavens to take me above!

Because they want me to do a favor
For some old fools,
Will eat me out of house and home...
For they hate to follow rules!

Why should I sit hear...
Just so nice and quiet?
While they eat everything up...
And cause in my house a riot!

And then what next?
What else would start looking good?
But this whole house
I should pick it up and move!

But where could I go?
Except the place that Moses stood...
For they wouldn't cross desert...
Because they'd die of thirst before they moved!

If they were all sponges
They'd soak stuff up...
They'd soak up whatever grub I have
And take it out of my house!

They want to play around
So close to forever...
Then turn around and eat all day long...

No matter what the weather!

Where are the good folks,
Who earns their way,
But these kids just wanna take,
And think they are earning their pay!

Why can't what I do in my house
Be just so quiet and private?
Because the grub I eat
Seems to keep the sky lit!

I wish the neighbor
Was the ice-cream man...
He would pick them all up...
And take them out of my hands!

And now I've had enough
To turn my head away...
I'm gonna fight fire with fire...
Or give them their way!

But what's this outside me window?
And what could it be?
Nothing short of a miracle
But the biggest apple tree!

So I stood their in awe
And went to see if I got
Not one basket, but two...
To carry them out!

And for all they stood there
For the grub I got...
When I find them two baskets

I'm gonna carry them out...

It took me a while
Searched high and low...
And there they was them baskets
Right behind my door!

I carried them outside
And climbed up the tree...
And I filled up them baskets...
Just for them to be happily watching me!

As they look up in wonder
I possess all the joy,
To invite these kids in,
To eat till they can't no more!

As they look up in wonder
From the top to the bottom of the tree...
Their eyes filled with joy
And they smiled at me!

And there I left them
To sit in the sun...
To eat till their hearts content
And boy, was they having fun!

And I know this for a fact...
This problem was just one...
That I never thought I'd solve..
Till I looked and seen the sun!

HIP HOP HUSTLE

Hip hop hustle!
Glory to the muscle!
That made it all happen...
experiences just for rapping!
And you knew that
dancing was here to stay...
All work-no play-
Gonna make you change
your ways...!

Hip hop hustle
Glory to the muscle
That made it all happen...
fingers toes are tapping
And tapping to the beat
It was the beat of the streets!
And for the lessons
you learned along the way
Like no pain no gain,
And it makes you wanna say...
You got to see it!
To believe it!
You got to feel it!
And you got to start dreaming it!
See it...
Believe it!
Feel it...
Dream it!
Hip hop hustle

Glory to the muscle...
That made it all happen...
The music, the beats
Made for rapping!

To the music, to the beat,
Shake, shake, shake!
To the music, to the beat,
Shake it to the east...
Shake it to the west...
Shake it to the very
Ones that you love the best!

Hip hop hustle...
Glory to the muscle!
I say Hip Hop Hustle!
Glory to the muscle!
And you knew that

Music was here to stay –
Learn life's lessons...
Try to change your ways
change your ways...
Here's how it stands:
If it's music you must make..
Then try to be positive and
A strong rapping man!
See it, believe it!
Feel it, dream it!
See it, believe it!
Feel it, dream it!
Hip Hop Hustle!
Glory to the muscle!
That made it all
Happen...experiences

For rapping...
Snapping my fingers...
Stomping my feet-
To the music
To the rhythm
To the rhythm
To the beat!
Snapping my fingers.....
Stomping my feet-
To the music
To the rhythm
To the rhythm
To the beat!

COMMON KILLER

Common killer,
Common saint,
Common killer-

The devil's not a saint!

Common killer,
Common saint,
Is what you believe in...

The common saint!?

Good God!
Good gold!
Thank Nguensta!

Because here I
Come-stah!

I create the rhymes
So you can feel the
Rushes!

Get ready for the world,
you and me...

Get ready for the world,
it's my pearl, see?

I sing
I sang
I sung
though here I come,
it's the real place to be....

I sing
I sang
I sung!

I ain't crying!
I am trying! to be just me!

I ain't crying!
I am trying! to be
totally free!

If it's fish! I'll scamper out and
buy it...If it's fish! I will fry it!
Fry fish! Fry you! Surely,
you must have a clue!
As to
what I'm doing here...
My rhymes are here to
stay...
The dirty dozen plus one...
I'm slap-happy in my own
standing family way!

Common killer
Common saint
It's so hot...that I
just might faint!

To have this gift is great

The African land is good
We thank the Living God
For the knowledge is our food!

Paint me a beautiful river
-Started by a stream-
Paint me a beautiful river
though as impossible as
it may seem!

There is nothing impossible
unto you...
There is nothing impossible
for You! You! You!

Common killer...
Common saint...
Common killer...

That's why the devil's
just not a saint!

CHANGE

Ever since the day we met,
Dawn of a new day arising,
The saying is still not so very strange,
Except I'm sitting here waiting for my man to change,

School days for the life of me,
School days for the twice of me,
Sitting here together we rearrange,
All the while sitting here waiting my man to   change.

Bet on a dummy and loose all your money,
Fools always want to disarrange,
They want dollars for no common sense,

Wait your change
Don't rearrange...

Wait your change
Don't rearrange...

Nothing's far from the honest truth,
I'm facing it just like Ruth,
Nothing's far from the honest truth,
I'm standing here facing it
Just like Ruth...

Because I'll have gray hairs
And grow old till I was dead-
Waiting for you to come out your cheating ways...

Because you'll never find me
Waiting up for you
And God knows the day
When and If you change...

Quit trying to rearrange...
Or just change!

You say that what the world needs
Is love sweet love?

Wait your change,
Don't rearrange...

Wait your change,
Don't rearrange...

You say what the world needs
Is love sweet love?

Wait your change,
Don't rearrange...

Wait your change,
Don't rearrange...

Because when and if you call...
Don't try to rearrange!

Since it's outta sight outta mind,
You can wait your 'cotton-picking' change!

When and if you call...
Don't try to rearrange!

Since it's out of sight, out of mind,
You can wait your 'cotton-picking' change!!

LAWNMOWER NOISE

Growing and growing
and going gallore...
Growing and growing
So give me some more...
Come back, boogie-woogie blues...
And show me what you got
In store...

All the right moves,
All the right grooves,

Is what you got in store...
All the right moves?

All the right grooves,
And all the right moves,
Hearing that lawnmower noise...
Waking you up
from a snooze!

Lawnmower noise as he
passes her by...
Lawnmower noise
He plans on the sly!

All the right moves,
All the right grooves...
Taking you up,
Waking you up,

Shaking you up blues!

Fade to black
Back to screen...
Save the drama for
Your mama
And you know what
I mean...

Save the drama for
Your mama...
Writing prose that's
Really mean...
Somebody's got to do it-
And that's me!

Give you,
Serve you,
Some boogie-woogie blues!
While hearing that
Lawnmower noise...
Puts you out of
the mood!

Lawnmower noise,
Lawnmower noise,

Hearing that
Lawnmower noise...
Waking you up
From a snooze!

Because temptation
and curves are
steadying his nerves,

So give the mistro
Some nitro, just like
friends and lovers should!

Put a band-aid on a blister,
Because them boogie-woogie blues
Can't miss ya'!

Genuine Moses...
No one knows this...was the affair...
Saint turned into skeezer,
So that men can go
To pieces...
While picking themselves up
The people, places and things,
And only the righteous!

Scratch and sniff first...
Dreaming again
So that hangovers
won't hurt!

Growing and growing
And going gallore...
Growing and growing
Louder than lawnmower noise
them boogie-woogie blues
are knocking down
opportunities and doors...

So strive
Arrive!
So I can
Give you some more!

TWO

We're two...
Soldiering
Birds of a
Feather and
Yes, we all
Stick together
Like two peas
In a pod...
I know I've got
A hot bod-

Who's to say?
Who's to deny?

These things won't
free you if
They're all lies...

That's my name
so don't wear it out!
The uncle- tomstress'
Likes to sing and shout
Nothing but insults...
If the shoe fits
She's gonna wear it....
Miss 'em diss 'em...
And also his clout!
While making you feel
So brand new...

Wanna hear my
Broken record?
That's news you can use...
Wanna hear my
broken record?
Hears news to relay!

Because two...
Soldiering
Birds of a feather
Like a team...
They always stick together....
Like two peas
In a pod
I know I've
Got a hot bod-
That's my name
So don't wear
It out-

Have to be careful
Have to have a plan!

So that we don't fear
the bounds!
Or be teetering on the edge!

fatal attraction sits on
a ledge

Waiting... for cupid to
nod yes... to send it
On it's way-
To us...as two lovers
tread ...
into the sunset...
to live forever
Until two lovers are dead!

SAINT TURNED SKEEZER

Saint turned skeezer
Pretend or do you
Believe her?
Who would have known...
It's a lie outgrown!

Saint turned skeezer
Nothing but a teaser
Who would have known
Unless you didn't keep
your own

In check--
No man had a hard time
getting respect...
Unless you didn't keep
your own
in check--
There wasn't no man
who was a saint
wouldn't believe her!
She just saint...
And at night
She's a skeezer!

Would turn men on
Would turn men off
With lavish spending
And fast cars at night

By day around of golf!

She says it's just a notion
I've gotta mind deeper
than the ocean!
And that's a natural fact
She said devil get back
Wanting to do what's right...
Misfortune is always at arms
length
And prosperity out of mind
Out of sight

I've got a mind that's deeper
straight hair is when
you receiver!

Saint turned skeezer...
Pretend or do you
Believe her?
Who would have known ...It's a lie out grown!

ROWING MACHINE

Stowing,
Knowing,
Showing,
Growing,
Rowing machine!
Like two peas
In a pod,
And you think it's
mean!
Furious, word to
the mother!
Your own prodigal
brother!
A wiff of fresh air...
It's not bitter
Or bare,
Differences of opinion
Brains: God gave you some!
So use them!

Stowing, knowing,
Growing, showing,
Rowing machine!
Is twice the competition
And you think it's a dream!
Over oceans and streams,
though impossible as
It may seem...

Real is our love
Love is our real
As white as a dove
Like a hand in a glove
We fit together...
Through all kinds
Of weather!
Two of a kind...
Gonna make you mine
Two loaves...
Five fish...
Yes two loaves,
And yes! It was a miracle
In love all is fair!

Racing ahead
Never being misled,
Miracle worker!
Like no amo-other!

It's smooth as silk,
And never to bilk,
folks out of millions...
Because I'm a person...
Ten to one zillion...
I'm a person-not one
One the world, but living
Amongst millions

Don't you want to go there
Streets of gold...
Diamonds and pearls
We all love to wear...
Seek higher learning
As high as eagles soaring!

Seek higher learning
And you will be growing!
He connected water

To dry land
Heaven is above
the earth,
as we all
Understand!
Gonna shake it!!
Because I'm gonna make it!
He's got a master plan!
You gotta leave it in His hands!
He's got a master plan
And a master mic-
While thunder rolls and
lightening strikes!
That parted the red seas!

Stowing, going,
Knowing, showing,
Rowing machine!
Like to peas in a pod
and you think it's mean!

REAL

If it's not real
We must conceal
If it's not in the brain
We must contain!

No pain
No gain
No pain
We must contain

No shots
No loss
No shots
Come count
The costs

To change-
Our hopes rearrange
The costs-
In you the Amozula
In the land of no
Winter frost!

If it's not real
We must conceal
If it's not in the brain
We must contain!

No pain

No gain
No pain
We must contain

No shots
No loss
No shots
Come count the costs

LIVE LOVE

Live, love
Laugh out loud...
While heads are up
walking tall and
speaking proud!

Live loud
Die proud
Give until it hurts...

Live loud
Die proud
Show loves worth...

worth seeing
worth believing!

All things become
brand new
One heart made two
He leads me into directions
No inhibitions
Or imperfections

Live,love,
Love live!
Live loud
Die proud!

Give-
Til it hurts
While the waves roar
loudly and while
the surfers take off
their shirts!

Live, love,
Love-live...
Hold on to the beauty
That you got to give!

Way up north
Or way down south...
Give all you can
Or just shut
your mouth...
Open it to reason
If you think
This is tough
Just call it treason!

Love live
Give what you got
Because you got giving
When the going gets rough!

HORSE

If I had a horse
It would say a whole lot...
If I had a thirst
That would hit the spot

Take a ride
Or wade in the ravine!
Venture on the Nile
Or jump through a stream!

I can't speak on it'....
Walking in new shoes....
Just go on and take them!
And hold on until it gives
You the blues!

IT'S GONNA MAKE YOU SURE!
THAT YOU WON'T HOLD BACK!
AND THEN YOU ARE DOWN...
MAYBE ENDING UP IN A SHACK!

This is what I'm saying to you:
What I'm relaying to you is true...
That's a natural fact...
NO I would lie to you
You took that!
Now see how hard it is...

TO WALK IN MY SHOES?

Now see how easy it is...
When I start to giving

YOU THEM BLUES!?
BUT WHEN YOUR TROUBLE COMES...
JUST KNOW WHERE IT WILL TAKE YOU!!!!

FEET BRAND NEW

I like the way
the crowd roars
when he comes
dashing through
the doors!

Drive yourself!
Revive yourself!
Life is a chore...
Sweet blessed Jesus

Open up some doors!

Feet brand new
Hands brand new...
Why wait?

Feet brand new
Hands brand new-

I'm safe!

DREAMBOAT

It's you!
Poetry is you!
Light the sky up
Because the stars are blue
And my days are sunny

No life without flowers...
Climbing tall towers...

Clothing the young ones
From head to toe
Making sure they fed
Never let 'em be misled

If you never getting
Nothing in return...
If the bun's not taken
Out the oven- it burn!

Dreamboat, steamboat,
Don't shake ya' head

Dreamboat,steamboat,
All the mouths must be fed!

Somehow, some way,
You had some fun
For a roll in the hay...

For a little
Heaven on earth drug...
For a sweep under the rug...

Patience once a virtue
But no longer today...
The guilt will mount
Hope will wither away

Like dead flowers
Dreamy, fine...and
Tall like towers!

Are you for real?
Or are you fake?
All it takes is once
Then it all be a mistake

Are you for real
Or are you fake?

Baptize,realize,
That heaven won't wait!

For a dreamboat, steamboat,
to get straight!

WISDOM

The wisdom to see,
The knowledge to know...

That old motherland,
That old motherland...

See her grass gardens,
And watch how they grow...

That old motherland,
That old motherland...

Beat the drums fast,
Beat the drums slow...

That old motherland
That old motherland...

Dance to the rhythm,
Move on with the show...

That old motherland,
That old motherland...

Watching my gardens,
And watching me grow...

That old motherland...
That old motherland...

UGLY CATS

I turned around and what did I see?
It was a bunch of ugly cats
Was just looking at me!
It was a bunch of ugly cats
Was just looking at me!
I turned around
and what did I see?
One eye-No eye...
No hair-don't care!
Three legs, peg-legged...
Their alienation...
Grumpy and bumpy
and fed up with starvation!
For not one year, but two!
They been sitting there so long
That they ain't know what to do...
But now it has come to this...
I have to get to the store,
And it's me against an army of cats

Somebody has shipped them to my shore!
They were born to stretch
And multiply from one to one million!
So just keep on feeding them
Have to start and keep breeding them!
But now it has come to this...
Have to let the story end or go on...
It's ten times Rembrandt!
And then they were gone!

But now it has come to this...
Have to let the story
End or go on...
It's ten times Rembrandt!
And then they were gone!

TRAIL BLAZERS

If ever you wonder
How I be...
Expressive, wonderful, giving...
That's me!

I live life
Love-live...
I love the beauty that she gives...

I love the rain
I love the snow
Just giving you the best
Just knowing what's in store...

If ever you wonder
How I be...
Expressive, wonderful, giving...
That's me...

I live life
Love-live...
I love the beauty
That she gives...

I love the rain
I love the snow...
I love what she gives
And then some mo'...

Give me some more seasons
And I'll give you so more reasons...

Take my hand
To the promised land...

Take my hopes...
And give me something dope...

Take my hand
To the promised land...

Make me free...
Make me believe!

THE BARONESS LIZZY

The Baroness Lizzy,
Lizzy to the bore,
The Baroness Lizzy,
Don't speak no more,
You go south to east,
And east to west,
You spend each day,
Knowing what is best!
The Baroness Lizzy,
Lizzy to the bore,
Folks downtown don't
Want you to take it no more!
She sees what she sees,
It is what it is…
But the mobsters got her
All wrapped up in they bizz'…
Baroness Lizzy,
Lizzy to the bore…
Ruling the underworld
Till they speak no more…
Baroness Lizzy,
Lizzy to the bore…
Ruling, and schooling
Till they hear it
No more!
Baroness Lizzy-
The Baroness Lizzy Lore!
Her house-her castle…
Tongues wagging

They pants sagging...
Baroness Lizzy,
Lizzy to the bore!
Speak to their conscience
Till they hear it no more!
Baroness Lizzy,
Lizzy to the bore...
See it - believe it
Dream it- scheme it
No more!

STRUTTING MY STUFF

I plunge forward and take a dive in the pool of life
I find food, clothing and shelter
From gray clouds of a fools frivolousness
Loom ground to sky
And all around...
One to choose and one to make a choice...
Just see what's in store for you...
I've got a smile turned upside-down
And the suns so big
It's gonna wash away all my cloudy days...
Turn rainy days into sunny ones...
Got a smile so big I put it on the sun ...
So the sun's got a smile and eyes like mine
I'm gonna turn around, turn grapes into wine...
Fill all the clouds with rainbows
So that your empty head can be filled with dreams...
Fill all the earth with beauty and precious things...
So your head can empty out its schemes...
Every bit of happiness is heaven to me...
I'll cheer for you and you'll cheer for me...
I'd rather love him than leave him
He makes me feel lovey-dovey, girly-wurly, see...
Because the more I learn to outsmart them fools...
The more them backstabbers will burn
With jealousy, with rage, with hatred for to learn...
Save what you want and save the best for last...
Because my life is not a stage
And you show ain't gonna watch

So just get the hell on off your but!

So are you gonna get off your butt and leave?
Why don't you just strut-
To the next town, city or state...
By plane, train or automobile,
Before you find yourself in concrete shoes...
And yourself in a big rut...
And when the door is open
I'll have a song in my heart
When the door is shut
I'll be so happy
Wouldn't know where to start!
I'll get up and strut...
I'm gonna strut my stuff!
I'll keep a song in my heart
I know just where to start...
Because this is a gem of an opportunity
I'm gonna strut my stuff...
And if you don't like it
Then so what...
Just mind your own business, see...
I'm gonna keep strutting my stuff!

THE DREAM

Sam had a laid back mansion,
And had a limo long, black, and sleek,
And had a garage to fit all of them,
Larger than next week!
Oh, how sweet life is for these
Rich folk,
Never wanting for nothing,
So I walk over to Sam
To pay him a compliment or something...
He invited me to dinner,
An evening drive
Were our plans for the day,
But he turned around to look at me
With such an evil face,
I had to get away!
I ran fast and swift,
Resentment I did harbor,
But the house went from grandoise,
To haunted funeral parlor!
The limo turned to hearse!
Didn't know which was worst!
Feeling so much fear and dread,
For in a mome

nt I'd be dead...
I knew I couldn't turn to fight,
For I felt so much fright,
The fear I felt
I could not tell...

The mansion turned to house
in hell!
But pretty soon I learned my lesson well,

Be careful what you wish for...

Some dreams are a hard, cold, sell!

SAMOSEAM

Samoseam! is the beautiful dream,
and the beautiful
dream of you!
It's the beautiful view-
And the beautiful dew-
And the things I do for you!
It's the beautiful scheme-
And the beautiful dream-
And the beautiful wonders
of what life can be-

Samoseam! is the beautiful
dream...and the beautiful
dream of you!
It's the beautiful view-
And the beautiful dew-
And the things I do for you!
It's the beautiful scheme-
And the beautiful dream-
And the beautiful wonders of
what life can be!
Samoseam- the beautiful dream...
Samoseam- the beautiful scheme...

THE CREED

Once, twice is an amazon...
Once, twice to play this song!
Once, twice, singing one, two, three!
Once, twice, because I aim to please...
Once twice is an amazon!
Once, twice just singing my song!
Once, twice, and you were once there.....
Once, twice, and I did not care...
Once, twice, what folks thought of me...
Once, twice, and all there is to see...
Once, twice, all there is to being me!
Once, twice, it was just you and me...
Once, twice, we both aimed to please!
Once, twice, from shore to sea!
Once, twice, is an amazon...
Once, twice just singing my song...
Once twice singing one, two, three...
Once, twice, and all to being me!
Once, twice is an amazon...
Once, twice, just singing my song!

Once, twice, and you were once there...
Once, twice, and I did not care...
What others thought of me...
Once, twice, because this is the creed!

PIPE DREAMS

Pipe dreams,
Pipe dreams,

More of a piper-sniper!

Pipe dreams,
Pipe dreams,

Something of a

Pleasure delighter!

Schemes, not dreams,
Are having their way,

Because have-not
Ain't got
For years of dismay!

Pipe dreams,
Pipe dreams,

Bet on a dummy...

Pipe dreams,
Pipe dreams,

Lose all your money!

Sit there and wait...
As you build up more hate...

You wear a weave...
Because you wanna receive...

    Pipe dreams,
    Pipe dreams,

Forget to remember...

    Pipe dreams,
    Pipe dreams,

Speedy December!

    Pipe dreams,
    Pipe dreams,

Are having their way...

    Pipe dreams,
    Pipe dreams,

Are having their say!

    Pipe dreams,
    Pipe dreams,

See it and believe it...

    Pipe dreams,
    Pipe dreams,

Straight hair is when

You receive it!

Pipe dreams,
Pipe dreams,

More of a piper-sniper!

Pipe dreams,
Pipe dreams,

Something of a
Pleasure delighter!

Schemes, not dreams
Are having their way...

Because have-nots
Ain't got-
For years of dismay!

Be there
Be Square
Be Low
Be Whole

Be There
Be Square
Be Whole

PERSON

I'm just a person
One in one million!

I'm just a person
Ten to one-zillion!

Here I stand
Though I'm not tall

The more you build up...
The higher the the great fall!

I'm just a person
Ten to one-zillion!

I'm just a person
One in one million!

Here I stand
Though I'm not tall...

There's nothing in the world
I won't do for you at all!

I'm just a person
One in one million

I'm just a person
Ten to ten-zillion!

Here I stand
Though I'm not tall

There's nothing in the world
I won't do for you at all!

THE WORLD

The word is pleasing
to the senses
and sounds tempting
to the ears

Like drugs can get
you high to believing

And make you feel
so damn good receiving!

Until-It makes your whole head spin!

Makes me feel
so damn low-
why you walking so slow-

Makes me feel
so damn low-
drama is like a show!

Makes me feel
so damn low-
why you walking so slow-

Makes me feel
so damn low-
drama is like a show!

The word is pleasing
to the senses
and sounds tempting
to the ears

Like drugs can
get you high
to believing,

And makes you feel
feel so damn
good receiving...

Until it makes
your whole
head spin!

Makes me feel
so damn-low!
Why you
walking so slow?

Makes me feel
so damn-low...
drama is like
a show...

Makes
me feel
so damn-low
Why you
walking
so slow?

Makes me
feel so
damn-low...
drama is like a show!

ONE ACE

I got big trouble, big love
from the heavens above

is where cupid come from
then he drum-beat-drum!

His arrow shot me...
then he up and got me!

Two hearts one ace
Then a smile on his face...

He laughed at me shuck
it all...once it was elusive...

it was far, far, far...

Now hear it come nearing
at the doors...

I don't want to know
despair no more!

These waves can't
hold no weave!

As we remember the
things we're about to
receive!

Drum beat drum....
say you sway...
And he up and got
Two hearts one ace!

Drum beat drum
say you sway...

And he up and got...
Two hearts... One Ace!

MAN HANDS

Man Hands...NO Indian giver...

Man Hands...Who'll ever out live her?

Your uncloudy nights
Turn dark skies from gray...

Your uncloudy nights...
Dance all your troubles away!

Man Hands...No Indian giver...
Man Hands...From hand to hand,
From river to river...

Man Hands...For the people
Hath given her...

Man Hands...One to cross the sea...
Another to cross the river!

Man Hands...Something you dare
Not say...

Man hands...Something you can
Relay...

Was one to rule ten million-
Something to make your day!

Man Hands! Always knew what
To do!

Man Hands! Like the moon, casts
A shadow over you!

Man Hands! You looked and saw
her standing there!

Man Hands! Will take you out
Of evils snare!

The troubled sea!
The troubled past!
The troubled sea...
To the rescue at last!

To bring you in headstrong!
To sing you a brand new song!

Man Hands! Forget your troubles
And past!

Man Hands! She's here at last!

Man Hands! NO Indian giver!
Man Hands! Who'll ever out live her...

Your uncloudy nights
Turn dark skies from gray!

Your uncloudy nights
Dance all your troubles away!

It was Man Hands...

The Indian hero!
It was Man Hands...
Won war after war!

Man Hands! The Indian
Warrior...

Man Hands! Who stands
Beside her...?

Man Hands...You'll never
Find another...

Man Hands...That was closer
To you than your own brother!

The troubled sea!
The troubled past!
The troubled sea
To the rescue at last!

The troubled sea!
The troubled past!
The troubled sea...
To the rescue at last!

Man Hands! Not your average
Leader...

Man Hands! Lived far away
And long ago!

Man Hands! Who is the greatest
Mystical ruler that you'll ever
remember and know?

Man Hands! Folks haven't
Heard enough...

Man Hands! Put the T in tough!

Man Hands! No Indian giver!

Man Hands! Who'll ever out live her?

Your uncloudy nights
Turn dark skies from gray...
Your uncloudy nights
Dance all your troubles
Away!

Man Hands! NO Indian giver!
Man Hands! Who'll ever out live her?

Your uncloudy nights
Turn dark skies from gray...
Your uncloudy nights

EASE ALL YOUR TROUBLES AWAY!!!

MAKE YOU WISH THAT YOU WAS

The music to the beat
The rhythm is your drug
The music to the beat
Make you wish that you was-

To the music
To the rhythm
To the rhythm
To the beat

To the rhythm
To the music
To the music
To the beat

Make you wish that you was
An unhappy maiden
Married to a spinster
Make you wish that you was
Take two and two together
And mix them-

To the music
To the rhythm
To the rhythm
To the beat

To the rhythm
To the music

To the music
To the beat

I love the music
The music just in me
I love the music
To the rhythm to the beat

Make you wish that you was
The rhythm is your drug
Make you wish that you was
The rhythm is your drug-

To the music
To the rhythm
To the rhythm
To the beat

To the rhythm
To the music
To the music
To the beat

The music to the beat
The rhythm is your drug
The music to the beat
Make you wish that you was.

OLD MAN RIVER

Sitting, wondering all their nights...
Being carefree all their days...
Freedom was the
Fight of all fights-
The right of all rights...
I'm gonna go tell it,
Go to the mountain...
For old man river
Took their tears
Wiped it off their faces...

God will as God will it!
Their freedom they
Was given it!
This was the story
That they told
They sat there thinking
Old man river
Had them sold
This was the story-
Of old man river-
This was the story-
Of the freedom
They been given-
And it seemed to take
Up all their time
Their freedom was given
For all times!
But what came next

Was the quiet storm
After the old man river
Freedom was the norm
They stamped out the devil
That made them perplexed
They stamped out the devil
Put them in hell with the rest
But don't put out the fire!
Made themselves comfortable
While taking themselves higher
With song-
The strong-
The young-
The old!

With song-
The strong-
The young-
The old!
Because old man river

Tried and true-
Took them to freedom
Under skies so blue!

THE TREE

The tree

Is unstressed

The tree

Is a test

A test of brains
A test of wits

For no soldier
Ever quits!

The tree is unstressed,

A test of brains,
A test of wits,

See what He has
In store for you,

For no soldier
Ever ever quits!

The tree
Is unstressed,

The tree

Is a test,

A test of brains,
A test of wits,
For no soldier
Never, ever quits!

The tree

Is undressed,

Stands mighty
And blessed,

Stands the best
For a perfect mind,

Stands the tree
And the sands
Of time for all Times!

MT. KILIMANJARO

But quietly I had
To slip away...
Not even less
Than a day...

So sound
Yet so gentle...
The winds may blow...
Almost swept me off-
Mt. Kilimanjaro!

So sad is
The inevitable goodbye...
See how grass grows
On my Mt. Kilimanjaro!

LIZZY'S BOREDOM II

Lizzy's Boredom-
Boredom- to- the- Lizzy!
Betcha- bottom-dollar,
Gonna love it in the city!
Yes, Boredom Lizzy
Is her name
Swinging and swaying
And singing is her game!

If you look and see her
She's far away...
But if you look again
She just might be there to stay!
Lizzy's Boredom
Boredom to the Lizzy!
His eye is on the sparrow
Flying high over the city!

BE THERE
BE SQUARE
BE HIGH
BE LOW

BE THERE
BE SQUARE
BE HIGH
BE LOW

LISTEN!

Listen!

To the sounds
Of the drummer man...

And his discovery of
an ancient land...

Yet
in his hands lie fate!

Better hear how they
slow down fast
At
his masters command:

Mon Khessan: Average Man!

Where the trouble begins-
Lusaka Ends!

Listen!

To the sounds of the
drummer man...
and his discovery of
an ancient land...

but in his hands

lie fate!

Better hear how
they slow down fast!
At his masters command:

Mon Khessan: Average Man!

Where the trouble begins!
Lusaka Ends!

Mon Khessan: Average Man!
Where the trouble
begins...

Lusaka ends!

KINKS

I got kinks in my
ankle-
like kinks
in your hair....
I got kinks like
your mama in
Gucci underwear!
I live for
them pops,
I live for
them kinks...
I live for the rhythm
just the way that
you think...
I live for the band...
I live for the plan...
I live for them kinks
For just the way
that you think!
If it's in the rhythm
then you can
get with them...
If it's in the
air then I
don't care!
Kinks in my hair
thinks I don't care...
Kinks not long-john
Gucci underwear!

Red light on stop
and green to go...
Red light on stop
just to Gucci you
some more!
Red light on stop
and green to go...
Red light on stop
just to Gucci you
some more!
Kinks making links
like they don't care...
Kinks making links
on Gucci underwear!
I live for them pops...
I live for them kinks...
I live for the rhythm
Just the way
that you think!
I got kinks in my ankle
like kinks in your hair!
I got kinks like your
mama in Gucci underwear!

THE DEED

See it!
Believe it!
Feel the dream...
See it!
believe it!
Instead of your schemes...

Try to make it plain,
Try to understand...
Feel no schemes...
Just live your dreams!
Feel no schemes,
Just living your dreams!

Breathe the air
Boogie-down
Gotta care!
And breathe the air
Boogie-down,
Gotta Care!

Of an ancient land...
Yet
In his hands
Lie fate!

Better hear how
they slow down fast!

At his masters command...

Mon Khessan!

Average man!

Where the trouble begins!

Lusaka ends!
Mon Khessan!
Average man!

Where the trouble
Begins...
Lusaka ends!

Amozeke! Amazon! Amo-Africans!

Searched high and low
All over the lands!

Like-

The A in Amo-Africans...
The M in Motunda...
The O in Oseikhu...
The Z in Zutundra...

The E in Effect...
The K in Korac
The E in Effect...

It makes you feel okay!

Mountain so high...
Valley so low...
Mountain so high...
To the river it flow...

Mountain so high...
Valley so low...
Mountain so high...
To the river it flow!

Amozeke! Amazon! Amo-Africans!

Reign-reign,
Reign-reign, all over
The lands!

Like-

The A in Amaze...
The M in Amazon...
The A in Amaze...
The M in Amazon...

The Z in Zulunda...
The O in Otumba...
The Z in Zulunda...
The O in Otumba...

AM-AM

ZO-ZO

How low can you go?!

AM-AM
Correct!

How high can you stretch?!

Amozeke! Amazon! Amo-Africans!
They ruled all over
The African lands!

Where the Ugah-Jugahs lived!
And the Ugah-Jugahs loved!
And the Ugah-Jugahs
Lived under the
Heavens above!

And listened
To the sounds
of the drummer man...

And his discovery...
recovery an ancient
Land...Yet in his
hands lie fate! In
his hands, why wait!

Better hear how
They slow down fast
At his master's command...
His masters command!
Mon Khessan!

Average Man!

Where the trouble
Begins !

LUSAKA ENDS!

Amozeke, Amazon
Of the African fate...

Amazon Mon Khessan
Of the average debate!

Amozeke, Amazon
Of the African fate!

Amazon ,Mon Khessan
Of the average debate!

Hand-in-hand...
From river to river!

From sea to sea
And hand-in-hand!
From sea to sea
I'm gonna say it again!

From sea to sea
And hand-in-hand
From sea to sea
I'm gonna say it again!

Amo,
Amo,
Africans!

Amo,
Amo-Africans!

the never-ending
rule all over the lands!

the never ending rule
while it's so grand!

MON KHESSAN: AVERAGE MAN!
WHERE THE TROUBLE
BEGINS...
LUSKA ENDS!

MON KHESSAN: AVERAGE MAN!
WHERE THE TROUBLE
BEGINS...LUSAKA ENDS!!!

AIN'T MISBEHAVING

My hearts broken
Is what I'm believing!
Ain't misbehaving
Like you receiving!
Down right dirty
And and able-believing!
Ain't misbehaving
Like you receiving!

There ain't no vitamin C
In that cup!
So stop acting like
There is...
Vitamin C ain't
Going out...
And ain't none
Coming in...
Deprivation is a sin...
You just can't
W - I - N...Win!
Seeing is believing...
That you ain't gonna be receiving...
Vitamin C ain't going out
And you can't put none in...
You just can't
W - I -N , win!

Why oh, why...
You just was the

Best!
Why, oh, why...
Is what I confess...

Dig a ditch,
Don't feel dismay,
Dig a ditch,
Just have it your way!

I say what you gonna do,
When it falls down on you?
I say, what you gonna
do, when those walls fall
Down on you?
Wait out the storm?
Or sit out your troubles
Like a princess in a
High tower!?

AFRICA

Where traders trade,
Where musicians play,
Where dances sway hips,
Where villagers move lips...

Where princes dwell,
Where kings rule by the bell,
Blue are her rivers,
Yet deep are her thoughts,
Many are her injustices,
The pearls of wisdom that costs...

The price of knowledge,
The price of beauty,
The price of shelter,
The stolen diamonds and rubies...

THE POWER

Flower Power!
Because they wanna take them all away...

Black Power!
Because we're here to stay...

Love Power!
Kiss and tell!

Woman Power!
Rule by the bell...

Knowledge is Power!
Your brain is like a sponge...

Man Power!
Do it and get it right!

Universal Power!
Power to those who believe it...

The Power!
'Straight hair is when you receive it!'

Universal Power!
Power to those who believe it...

The Power!
'Straight hair is when you receive it!'

Black Power
Of the hour...
Straight hair- you gotta
believe it!
Straight hair is when
you receive it...

Black Power
Of the hour...

Straight hair-you gotta
believe it...
Straight hair is when
you receive it...

Black Power
OF THE HOUR...
STRAIGHT HAIR-YOU GOTTA
BELIEVE IT...STRAIGHT HAIR IS WHEN
YOU RECEIVE IT!

DREAM, DREAM, FREEDOM's BELL

The higher you build
The higher your fall...

The stronger the will...
The more power for us all...

Dream, Dream, freedoms bell...
Dream, Dream, eat to live well...

Dream, Dream, Wait your
Change...

Dream, Dream
May even seem strange...

Behold!
Dream, Dream...

As difficult as it may seem...

Behold!
Dream, Dream...

From anywhere in between!

Dream, Dream
Freedom's bell...

Dream, Dream
Eat to live well!

DREAM

You know all I ever do
Is dream about you...
At night and at day...
In every given way...
The knights are at flight
With every sleepless night
Expressions flare!
Assume I care!

It's being specific
That keeps it terrific
It's the style of your hair...
It's the clothes that you wear...

You know all I ever do
Is dream about you...
At night and at day
In every given way...
The nights are in flight
With every sleepless night...
Expressions flare!
Assume I care!

It's being specific
That makes it terrific
It's the music you make
It's the rhythm you create
It's the clothes that you wear
It's the style of your hair

You move me
You groove me
You show me
You know me

Expressions flare!
Things you share!
How you dance for me...
How you chance for me...
How you walk with me...
How you talk with me...

Keep living
Keep giving
Keep being
Keep seeing

Keep dancing
Keep romancing
Keep seeing
Keep believing

EARL

Earl the pearl
The wisdom you took!
Earl the pearl
Write me a book!
Earl the pearl
So I can see!
Earl the pearl
Mean so much to me!
Earl the pearl
Like a bright sunny day!
Earl the pearl
Why don't you come my way!
Earl the pearl
If ever or never!
Earl the pearl
Through all sorts of weather!
Earl the pearl
Turn dark skies blue!
Earl the pearl
The many ways I show I love you!
Earl the pearl
You rock my world!
EARL THE PEARL-
THE PERIL!
THE WORD!!

FACING THE HONEST TRUTH LIKE RUTH

Getting to forget
Forgetting to get

To have and not to hold
To hold and not to fold

Giving to receive
Forgetting to believe

Anxious to make a bet
And so willing to receive

Facing the honest truth
Standing here with Ruth

Having somewhere to go
And going with the flow

Knowing you, knowing me,
Showing you where to go,
Showing you what I believe,

Just believe it...
So willing to receive it...

Nothing's farther than the truth...
I'm facing it just like Ruth...

Nothing's farther than the truth...
I'm facing it just like Ruth...

LONG GONE

You once was lost but
Now you're found...
Betcha bottom-dollar
Spent on the town...

You once were here
And now you're there...
Telling me a tale that's
Totally square!

Oh, sing us a song!
String us along...
Sing after we're long gone
And make merryment
On and On...

Long gone,
Long gone,
So far away...

Long gone,
Long gone,
Though you were
Here to stay!

Could it be the beginning
Of a brand new day?

Could it be the end

Of an old family way?

Fair-crossing you
From left to right...

Swinging and swaying
To a song such a wonderous
delight!

Could it be so wrong...
We are in the great race...

Could it be so wrong...
Scandal could be such
A total disgrace!

Long gone,
Long gone,

led astray...

Long gone,
Long gone,

Refusing the family way...

For the love of money
And all for status...

For the love of the honey
And everything that matters!

Long gone,
Long gone,

What's a person to do?

Long gone,
Long gone,

Just when you thought that
You knew...

Long gone,
Long gone,

Knew enough to know
about the family way...

Long gone,
Long gone,

Knew enough to show
Your faith and stay...

Long gone,
Long gone,

Right by my side all the way!

Long gone,
Long gone,

So far away...

Long gone,
Long gone,

That you might be
here to stay!

I MUST LEAD

Though I can be led
I must lead...
Because they will follow
I must succeed...
Gonna drive
And be driven...
No I won't waver
At the outer limits
Of the moons crater...
Though I can follow
I must lead...
They will not stay
But only stray...
I have no care
I have no worry...
Because a leader
Leads a tribe...
And tribes need a leader...

Lord lead me to a
Brighter day...
Because the good Lord giveth...
And He taketh away...

Though I can follow
I must lead...
North to Northwest..
West to Northeast...
Others can hope

What they cannot see...
No I won't lead
Those too scared
To follow...
The rest can have hope
And for a better tomorrow...

HAVE-NOT LESS-GOT

Stupid is
As stupid does...

Pretty is
Just what it was...

The more I give
The more you take...

When your
Trouble comes...

Just know for sure
What it makes...

Have-not
Less-got

Have-not
Less-got...

...To be such a showoff!

Stupid is
As stupid does...

Pretty is...
Just what it was...

The more I give
The more you take...

When your trouble
Comes...

Just know for sure
What it makes...

HOPE

Hope is the
One lone
Cry
In the wind...

That the devil
tempted Eve
to sin...

Peace be still
And peace
To you
Again...

Hope is the
One lone
Cry
In the wind...

HUNGRY THIEVES III

So now, what's this? You say...
It's a hungry thieves part three!
Well tell me, say it ain't so...
It just wasn't really meant to be!

So I'll put it this way...
And here's what I said:
At long, long last
Those hungry thieves are fed!

At long ole last
Twas a breath of fresh air!
Like a page from a story book...
In love and war, all's fair!

The memories rung a bell
And it gave you some laughs...
A story that serves you well
And gives you joy at long ole last!

Those hungry thieves I fed
They went from sup- to super!
It felt really really good
Once I turned them into my troopers!

There's no place like grub
When your house is a pub!
There's no place like grub
Make your house a pub!

I LIVE IN A WORLD

I live in a world...

And the world
goes around...

Where the hunted
And the hunter
Wears the pants
And something big is
Going down...

I live in a world...

And the world
goes round..

Change...

And give me change...

Come as you are...

Just stay the same...

FOR A LITTLE HEAVEN ON EARTH DRUG

I was born
I was raised

here on earth,

I was born
I was raised

'Came right from the dirt...

Oh yes, indeed
it's me in the need,

Found a quarter
in the dirt...

Blow it off don't hurt!

I'm here to stay-
I cry-I die!

Have to kill some bugs...

In a valley so high!

I squashed them devils
In the dirt...

found a quarter on the ground
but what was it worth?

Dog gone-gone dog
Play fair-Be square!

For a little heaven on earth drug-
For a little sweep under the rug-

For a little heaven on earth drug
In the bottomless pit up above!

Dog gone-gone dog
Make them devils disappear

Dog gone-gone dog
Show them no fear!

For a little heaven-on-earth-drug!
For the beauty up above

Show them no fear...
Fear them no show...

In the valley up above
For A little heaven on earth love...

I'm here to stay...
I cry, I die,

Had to crush the opposition
In a valley so high!

Valley so high
Valley so low...

Valley so high
To the river they flow...

Valley so high
Valley so low...

For a little heaven on earth drug...
For a little sweep under the rug...

For a little heaven on earth drug...
In the bottomless pit of love!

BRIGHT EYES

Bright eyes
As bright eyes blue
Warm embrace
And tender are you
When you're next to me
Are thoughts so real
Thoughts of loving you
And things which
Always do appeal...

I want you near to me
As you are dear to me
Take my hand
Let's go to the promised land
Take my hand
Not hard to understand...
So what's the big deal?
Is you rolling like a wheel?
And the heart of you's for real
And the heart of mine you steal...

ASHY

Ashy lips! need
constant zip!

Crabby old wooden legs

Crabby old wooden and she begs
For attention she wants
But wasn't getting none...

Trouble wouldn't come
Till she searched for some...

Fat, old clumsy hands,
Flying through sea, air, bodies, and land...

Button your cracked lips
And take your hands
Off your hips...

I want you to change
Quit trying to rearrange!

Your foolish ways
Will be the cause of your downfall!

A GIRL CALLED STUPID

A girl called Stupid,
is her name...
A girl called Stupid,
playing her game...

A girl called Stupid,
is her name...
A girl called Stupid,
Playing her game...

Once was lost,
But now she's found!
There's no more pretending-
She's heaven bound!
A girl called Stupid
Served her time well...
A girl called Stupid
Sometimes you can never tell...
If Judas wasn't a traitor
This I know for sure...
She used her time well...
But will love be the cure?

A girl called Stupid
With the glasses on her face...
A girl called Stupid
Is now a fighter for the human race!

A girl called Stupid

To change for a season of change
A girl called Stupid
Her time has come to rearrange!

A girl called Stupid
Stand once and for all
A girl called Stupid
Was no name to be called!

Stupid was bad
As we understood...
Stupid now fights for the common good!

A girl called Stupid
Is her name
A girl called Stupid
Playing her game
Once was lost
But now she's found
There's no more pretending
She's heaven bound!

THE TALK

Love hurts because Eve sinned...
Poverty exists because Adam gave in...
And took a bite from the apple
of the tree of knowledge of
good and evil!

So Adam took a bite,
He thought he was right,
Gods patience was worn thin...

So instead of coming out-
He going back in...

The closet is a walk-in...
Keep your baggage in there
And do what's right!

WIDER THAN THE RIVER

Amozeke! Amazon! Amozula!

Is not just a notion!

Amozeke! Amazon! Amozula!

Far and wide
all across the oceans!

The "A" in Amozeke
Wider than the river...

The "M" in Amazon
For the love the Motherland
has given her!

The "O" in Amozula
To keep us going strong...

The "Z" in Amozeke
Because you'll never forget this song!

The "U" in Amozula
Wider that the river...

The "E" in Amozeke
For the love the motherland had
given her!

The "Z" in Amazon
To keep us going strong...

The "Z" in Amazon
IN YOU THE AMOZULA!!!!

DREAMS AND DESIRES

My dreams are
Fading away
Fast!
I hardly
Have time...
Because dreams
Are like
Rare gems
And rare finds...
Once one
Has designs...

My true
Loves lorn
Lost...
Rare and
Fading away...
Count the
Cost...

What do I do?
Where do I go?
Seeds that you plant...
Seeds that you sow...

But what do I do?
Where do I go?
Seeds that you plant...
Seeds that you sow...

THE ESCAPADE

The escapade is all about
love, devotion, and honor...
And never betray what you follow!
Always forget and never remembering...
our hearts are made as one,
The oddities...
The drama has our hearts as one,
They hollowing us love inside,
When the evil creeps around
Why should we hide?
We should fight!
To try to put those things
Out of our sight!

Our sight,
So that they creep around...
The oddities,
Trying not to make a sound...

So before they turn back
And try to destroy the cause,
Put it in reverse
Or you better pause!
Nothing's gonna stop us now,
The drama!
Your mama!
May pop us loud...
Right side, upside the head
To keep common sense

Trapped in...
Locked in the brain instead...
If you can count,
You are prepared,
For the rain
So let it be never misled!

The escapade is about,
Love, devotion and honor
And never betray what you follow!
That's why we fight
The evil that creeps around quietly
And so-called, innocently,
Turns around to war against us
To fight
The drama,
Your mama,
The us!
Your mama is who you trust!
With all your life
so let it show
them whose boss!
Paying the price and
We paid the cost!

The oddities were following
Us all around...
For they seek to destroy...
After being kind, clever,
and coy!
And for that reason,
They seek to annoy...
So they need to get lost!
Coming out of their dead...
And still being misled,

It's the heart and the mind
that has died the death as well!
So the zombies seek,
So the zombies hide
Like a pack of soldiers
Waiting to jump out of hiding,
To come outside!
The pain
The joy,
The drama,
The ploy!
The us...The joy, in who you trust!
Seeking to destroy,
Persistence is a must
Insistence by those
who will only sit by and rust!
While they decide
Whether to fight or hide!
We're the pure!
We're the sure!
We're the hard-workers...
We have the cure!
And that's why...*WE WILL DESTROY THEM!!*

FOR REAL

Yours being lost in the cracks of society
Yours being tossed in the wind
Like a windmill-
Can't you see?
You were everything a brother
Should be-for real...
You were everything...
Once poor and pressed,
Now here's the deal...
Stressed or arrest,
The competition wore a vest...
Stressed or arrest,
There are witnesses who have
Seen the very, very, best!
The very best of them,
While your life is flashing by...
Isn't that what it's all about?
To give it the old college try
But if you'd rather die than cry...
Wait for real...
And change, then get changed...
And that's the deal-
No lie!
Rearrange the plan...
So your heart can feel
It beat again...
Better believe it!
Straight hair-don't care...
To better receive it!

Be for real,
My heart you steal,
Always at your best,
Whether poor, or pressed...
Be for real,
For real to be,
Not always suffering...
Because you're always tougher
And that's the deal!
Yours being lost in the
Cracks of society...
Yours being tossed in the
Wind, like a windmill...
Can't you see?

HATE

Hate: the illusion!
Rust: Until your brain is
a contusion!
This is what it makes you:
Hate until it breaks you!
Don't do it...
Or try to think
You can go through it...
Never let them see you sweat...
Become an achiever,
and you'll never have
any regrets!
Achieve!
So you can go forward!
Believe!
In the things people
get more of...
This is what it makes you...
Hate until it breaks you!
Got a mind to get through it...
So move!
It's not a suggestion!
Prove!
Is not the only question
That folks are going to have
For you...
Amozeke-believing
In all the hate....
Amozeke-receiving

All that is great!
Beauty but a curse...
Brains, but a reverse
In misfortune!
Giving you heck...
And putting you in a wreck!
Go through some pains,
Walk through the rain,
And while you're at it
Hope you feel forced
To do nothing but complain,
Go through it
Get on to it
Even though sometimes
It may not be much fun
Then folks will see
The inner beauty in me
The outward conspiracy
Which they try to reach
Hate is what it makes you
Hate until it breaks you!
Not last, not least,
Sad, ugly, sick or deceased!
I ain't dead,
I'm gonna get ahead,
Whose nickels and dimes
Are lost...
Dig them up and count the cost
Of the sacrifices
And the prices
That were paid for you!
Now is the time
To gather up and be strong
Not sit around and be blue!
Hate: the illusion!

Rust: Until your brain
Is a contusion!
This is what it makes you
Hate until it breaks you!
Do or don't
You will or you won't
Try to get on through it...
So be not a follower
Got to lead!
These things must free
your mind if you want to succeed!
Are You Ready?!

SPREAD LOVE

But if you want American music
I say
Pat Boone...
Spread the love
Spread the joy
Because God gonna come soon!
Sooner is better than later...
Or is it that you're a couch-potato?
Here I am
At last!
Here I am!
Soon, death will be a part of the past, so...
Take your phone off the hook...
And rest up with your favorite book.
Straight hair is when you're receiving peace...
The violence against us should just cease!

Better whenever you delay it...
Ideas that you can relate to
And never quit!
So it's better late than never, I say...
Free your mind before you under the dirt!
Got to always pray!
Prayer is the essence of survival
A perfect new life in the world
WAS HIS ARRIVAL!

Spread the love!
Spread the joy!

with tradition...
and Zeke-Ambition...
While building up nations
and closing life's doors!

And when you find the sun is
still shining rays and showers...
You will be amozeke-arriving
On trains and tall towers!
That gives the race cars speed,
while at that supplying all
your needs!
Yes the train was blue
Not a sad one,
but fast enough to make
you say: Glory- Hallelu!

How can you feel
It's just pretend?
That there aren't a lot of
Ways to tell a true friend...
So relax after a hard days work,
And folks won't go thinking
In their minds you're a jerk!
So who is the first?
The first and the last...
Erase all your worries
And let it be a thing of the past!

Spread love
Spread the joy
So that you can hear the story
Of the miracle baby boy!
You know the name,
You know the legend,

You know it's more
Than ancient history
And more than the luck
Of number seven!

Remember the first
Remember the last
Remember the traces
In your past!
SPREAD LOVE!
SPREAD THE JOY!
...With tradition...
...And Zeke-Ambition...
...While building up nations...
...And closing life's doors!

SPREAD LOVE!
SPREAD THE JOY!
...With tradition...
...And Zeke-Ambition...
...While building up nations...
And closing life's doors!

PERFECT WORLD

Why can't this be a
Perfect world??

Let this old one crumble
And come to an end!

Why can't this be a more
Perfect world...

Where despair and misery
Is not my constant
Companion and friend

It's the good one that got away!

So what's the use in trying
To stay in between a rock
And a hard place?

-Kept the faith while
Running this rat race

-Kept the faith while
Feeling this dark and
Dismal disgrace,

Separate but equal
In separate beds,

Separate but equal
Wishing for a paradise land!

A more perfect world
In a better place-

A more perfect world
Will end a rat race!

That had been going on
Since times past,

That had been going on…
So I could be freed
At last!

Time flies when you're
Having fun,

If I'm a worldly woman
I'm not the only one!

May have been stuck
In this rut or here to stay,

It still might all be pretend…
More than sunshine
On an uncloudy day!

But in this perfect world
I will find my place

Which will be where ever
I want…
So get out of my space!

Perfect world,
Perfect friend,

Perfect world,
Is it only pretend?

A more perfect world,
In a better place!

A more perfect world
Ended a rat race!!

GREATNESS FOUND

Greatness found
Greatness lost
Amozeking everything
You thought was boss!

Arriving at the solution
Is like being king!
Not cursed, but blessed
In everything!

Put it to the test
While never really
Laying it to rest

Put it on pause
And fight hard
For the cause!

When you have
The upper hand…
And fight hard
For the cause

Like you was
In the motherland!

I fight with a big
Stick…
Because my mama

Raised me like this!

Greatness found
Greatness lost!

And when you feel
So good
You're singing in the
Cold rain...

Just count the cost!

Greatness found,
Greatness lost,

Amozeking
Everything you thought
Was boss!

Arriving at the solution
Is like being king!
In answer to your question,
It recreates in you
The amozula in everything!

And making you turn
Every which way
But loose...

Greatness is only
Found in God's
Golden truth!

So when greatness
Is found

And greatness lost,

Just face the honest
Truth...
And you shall be boss!

You will arrive at
The solution
Which is like being king...

Not cursed,
But blessed in everything!

THE BLOOD

How do I know?
Because the blood told me so!
I said ask me how I know
Because the blood done told me so!
Just like Cain killed Abel
When he died
The blood didn't tell God no fable!
So he couldn't hide!
Nothing's far from the
Honest truth...
I'm standing here
Facing it like Ruth!
The blood can tell a lot,
Because a Lie will
Stay on a liars mouth.
The blood will tell
Because a liar is just
Going to fail you
Through in and throughout...
And let you down quick-
Don't forget Cain, and Abel...
Don't forget the stick!
If you only can see
The ugly truth and how it's
meant to be...
All a bad dream
And a thing of the past
All a bad dream...
But are we really free at last?

Be pure and true...
Let the music all blast ...
-you away-
As real as we can be...
I sent the cats out to play....
It's me, I'm free...
It's real, so why don't
You just let it be!
It's me, I'm free,
It's real...So why don't
You just let it be!

PERFECT FIT

Indirect, distant interpretations
Better tight-knit families,
Tribes and nations!
I've got the answers
I've got the key-
Faith is the weapon
Fear get to steppin', see…
Driving the answers
Out of your brain
So that we won't
Go insane!
Strength is what will
Drive you-it's the key-
I've got the answers
To all of your misery!
And let it be a perfect fit…
Like a new shoe
So be it…
Let it be a perfect fit-
Hope is the one lone cry-
We all need it!

OPEN ROAD

If a lie is the truth
And the truth is a lie...
I'd just as sure as fail
When I succeed
And be succeeding
When I fail to die-

For a worthless cause

I say youth is inner beauty
And someone says as much
As that Rudy...pause!
Because things are gonna
Be like that...
I'm still writing the
Kind of prose that rocks--
I'll be on the attack!

For a little heaven-on-earth drug
For a little sweep under the rug

For a little heaven on earth drug...

In the bottomless pit of love!

RAT RACE

This rat race,
This gangster pace,
Has always been
Where it's at,
Because they
Can't fight...
Can't get it right...
In this rat race dwelling
On the past!
They got back where,
They're supposed to be
Where, nobody can see
At last!

I'm tired-
Ain't going nowhere...
Better believe it...
I've got straight hair...
This rat race is always
Where you receive it!
Always stressed
But never impressed
I ain't dying or dead
Because the music
Because the rhythm
Had left things unsaid...
So go ahead
Complain to Fred
Why can't they get it right?

At last a breath of fresh air,
A blast from the past
Makes you go from slow
To full steam ahead!
So you can run this rat race,
Keep going the gangster pace,
And always know where it's at!

I can't complain,
To keep from going insane,
And always know where
It's at!

Gonna move mountains this time,
Gonna bust a stupid old rhyme,
Gonna make you feel the rhythm
For the truth we are always going
To be given...
Got to keep running this rat race
Got to keep up this gangster pace

Because that's always
Where it's going to be-
This old rat race!

PIGLATIN

Piglatin...

I'm making things happen,
Things are going to slow down,
Don't plan on stopping me now...

Don't go away mad,
Don't hang around-
Leave or be glad...
For the heaven-bound
For that virgin sound

Piglatin!

I'm making things happen,
Experiences for rapping,
So instead of coming out-
He's going back in
Just to be attacking!
And if you don't like it
You cease to know the deal...
Get to stepping out of my door

But be for real!

EDUCATED

Success is hell,
And poverty is heaven,
Six is the beast,
And yours the lucky
Number seven!
Because thugs and bugs
What you don't want to see...
Thugs and bugs
Only bring you misery!
Thugs, bugs and drugs
In your neighborhood...
Thugs, bugs and drugs
Ain't never going to
Be nothing that's good!
Everyone stressed,
Until we all become blessed...
Come together,
All birds of a feather,
So you can see...
That your history
Ain't no mystery
So
Get educated!

THE WINNING HAND

A thing of beauty
In life won't last

A thing of beauty...
Put the "T" in task...

If your life's a sensation,
Then I'll make headlines
And waves all over this nation!

Which dance floors are solid ground,
So that indecisiveness is virgin sound,
Make headlines for the cause today..
Get educated- go all the way!

Which do you choose
Which do you lose,

You've got to play your
Card hand right...
For whatever your fate is
Got to make a little educated guess

Live, love, learn...

Pass the test! Gain insight!

For it's the winning hand!

THE VIRGINS

Truth is a dare,
Take it or leave it…
Knowing God's legendary history,
Is when you choose to receive it!
Now the virgins had sticks
And the virgins had stones…
The virgins got them running scared,
So folks swore they'd leave them alone,

They went in with their sticks
To beat the devils down
Because devils got their kicks
Bringing them down!

And as they vowed to cheat old death,
The virgins got guns…
Because they wasn't working
For their health!

So they went into their own garden,
To see if the roses behaved,
Because the virgins are a mighty number…
Christian folk who never go astray!

So now that you know
The virgins, their numbers and the show…
Will always have folks running scared

So just leave them alone-

RIPER-VIPER PASTURES

Either the experiences
Are bitter...
Or they are sweet...
Riper-Viper pastures
Is such a bubbly, tasty, treat!

And it got you in a wreck
It's gonna give you heck,
It wasn't yours,
It was mine
Because we are two hearts
Made one
Two hearts got their lives!

These things must free your mind
If you wanna play- Are you ready?

For riper-viper pastures
Are you ready?

We're going home
We'll gonna fly away
And our pace is always steady!

BEEN BORN

I've truly been born
I've truly been sworn
To protect and serve

I'm torn
Been born
Why you wearing my pearls?

What are the words
Because I had forgotten them
To have you to hold you..
To wash, dry and to fold you...

Truly been born
I've been sworn
To silence and secrecy
And to heighten this legacy

I'm torn
Been born...
Juggling some dreams

I'm torn
Been born...
Cooking up some schemes

Juggling, smuggling, and struggling
To keep goals alive
Juggling, struggling, and struggling
To amozeke-arrive!

HIGHER PLANE

Bright-brained, educated and trained...
Bright eyes as bright eyes blue tamed...
He's revolutionized the world
And the worlds got to revolve
Into a hope brand new!
He's revolutionized the world
Into a place that's so brand new!

If you close your mouth
You wont have to holler
Stream, river stream,
Because the river runs opposite...
Chasing you
Embracing you
That's running wild
Was the excited child...

Bright brained,
Educated and trained,
Higher plane...
Jesus and God are One
And the same!

-Place He once was and is as before...
In that place called Eden
One day the angel blocked the doors...
Choose, don't lose
So that we can be winning-receiving...
Creation, the power and the glory

Means a whole lot more!

Because the end
Justifies the means
Will be different
Until busting out at the seams
Just waiting to receive you
Because this world is a stage...
Just wanting to believe in you
On a higher higher plane!

-Where there's room for both of us...
Brighten up the skies too much
-Where there's room for both of us
And the pipes are clean
Copper will always rust!

Choose, don't lose,
The power is us...
Choose, don't lose-
Your faith-or you'll only start to rust!

YOUR MIND

Your mind is a dangerous weapon
So if folks don't like how I relay it
Then folks can get to steppin'!

It's the hope where creation
Is all brand new...
It's the help where the word is bond
And the coward's eyes gets
Turned black and blue!

Shield and spear
Will protect you in your
Secret endeavor...
And that your hope in
Amozeke, Amazon Amozula

Is the new weapon!
Your Mind That Place!
Good God The Race!
Your Mind That Place!
Good God The Race!

Some say the imagination
Is a dangerous weapon
And as creation is made
The imagination is a dangerous weapon!
Peep this, keep this,

Or just get to steppin'!
Your Mind, That Place...
Good God, That Race!

Your Mind, That Place...
Good God That Race!

Your Mind, That Place...
Good God, The Race!

Your Mind, That Place...
Good God That Race!

THE YOUNG

The youth need only to realize
The young must truly recognize

We need to amozeke-strive,
So that we all can amozeke-arrive1

Us together, like birds of a feather
Let us all keep hope alive

The youth need only realize...
The young must truly recognize-

New hope
New dreams
One and the same
But so far and few in between!

The youth need only realize
The young must truly recognize

Eternal youth
Everyone wants it...

The eternal song
You're gonna want to sing
Dance and flaunt it!

For a little heaven and earth drug
For a little sweep under the run

In the bottomless pit of love!

The youth need only realize,
The young must truly recognize!

SNAKES AND THE LEGEND

Snakes and the legend
Yours, the lucky number seven...
Safer if you go north
Disgraced if you move south
Prosperous if you are east...
Honored, if you move west!

That is why number one is wise
These things must free your mind
If you wanna play...Are you ready?

Loyalty is what drives you
With straight heads
It's seeking to arrive with you...

Because some people
They don't understand
If we know our hearts..
Then we're always home,
In the motherland!

Snakes and the legend
Yours, the lucky number seven

Coming and going,
Learning while we are turning,
Every which way, but loose...

Yours the lucky number seven,
Snakes and the legend!

THE LOVERS

The lovers of the world are hopeless
It's tearing me apart going coatless!

But more and more I see the change
Shipped to shore
Oh, how they rearrange!

The world needs to adjust
But more and more
I see the change
Or, God, we rust!

You're all that's fine,
Footloose and fancy free
And all that's original
Making eternal history!

You're all that is simply wonderful
That's why I'm feeling, being free
You're all that's simply wonderful
That's why I feel no misery...

The lovers of the world are hopeless
It's tearing me apart going coatless!
But more and more I see the change
You're all that's fine, footloose and
Fancy free-

Try to rearrange!

WANTED

Seeking a different
Kind of artist
With a different kind
Of vision

Seeking a different
Kind of world with
A bolder kind of wisdom-

Who was it
Who does it
On the right road
All the way home!

Who was it
Who does it
On the right road
All the way home!

Walking to the beat
Of a different drum
Seeking someone who
Walks hand-in-hand

With sticks for a drum!

To the beat,
To the rhythm
Of a drum-beat-drum

To the beat
To the rhythm
Of a son-of-a-gun!

Seeking a different
Kind of Artist
With a different kind of vision

Seeking a different kind
Of world with a bolder kind
Of wisdom!

BETTER DAYS

Better days are coming soon
If you don't like what I'm saying
Then look at the moon!

Better run this race
Must take first place
Because you'll never finish the run
If you don't wake up-
Then you'll miss the morning sun!

Let's free our minds
Because we wanna play,
Soon is soon
For a bigger, and brighter day!

Hands off the drag queen
Hands out of the cookie jar
Or you'll make the drama mean-
So much more in pictures
Than words can express
So much more in pictures
Than words help to pass the test

Believe
Better days are coming like rain

Receive
Because bad dreams can
Drive a person insane!

Keep running that race
-Must take first place
Better days are coming soon
As the world goes round the sun
When you walk into the room!

Relate!
Don't hesitate!
Arrive!
We must survive!

Don't stress
But try and pass the test,
And there won't be no repulsions...

Believe
Always receive
Instead of going into
Convulsions!

Better days are coming fast
If you don't believe what I'm saying
Then get out of the past...

Wake up out of your sleep,
And just turn over a new leaf,
Blaze a trail and forge a path...
Blessings you receive
Always free at last!

Soon to come are better days
So go ahead and let the haters rage!
Be a winner
Not always a beginner

Strive fast!
Death will be a thing
Of the past...

Be a winner
Not always a beginner
Strive fast!
Death will be a thing
Of the past!

THE JOY

Life's a hero sandwhich
With a brassy, sassy song…
Wa'tusi on Lucy
Singing it all night long!

All the joy Watissimo!
If you blink
You miss it more!

What is it except
Another bad creation
What is it except

Living, laughing and loving
In God's glorious elation!

All the joys of life's despair,
Innocent until proven guilty
Because a white lie is
Only a snare!

All the joy Watissimo!
If you blink
You miss it more!

A FINER LINE

A much finer line
Between good and evil
A much happier time
With the people you
Believe in...

It's the quickest,
It's the hippest,
Amozeke-receiving...

It's the quickest,
It's the hippest,
All that is worth perceiving!

A finer line,
A happier time,
For the folks you
Believe in,
Who are always
Amozeke-believing!

A finer line,
At the fastest pace,
A finer line,
In order to finish this race!

More hope to come,
Soon your work is done,
Achieving more dreams

That you can reach,
A little heaven on earth drug,

And a finer line,
So let's keep trying,
-To teach!
About a new world renown
So that only the world we can see!

A FINER LINE part 2

Some say that the mind
Is a dangerous weapon...

So you can either peep this
Or get to steppin'!

A finer line is a better place
A finer mind good God
The race!

A finer line between
Love and hate,

A finer line because
Heaven won't wait

A finer line between
Good and evil

A finer line can only
Make you a believer!

GIVE IT A REST

What you get out of hard work
Is success...
Keep on striving
Keep on arriving
Or just give it a rest!

Because they are building
You up just to tear you down...
They are building you up,
So that they can always
Hang around...

Rome wasn't built in a day
If I say leave
Then you best not
Try to stay!

And when it was burnt down
They had to try and survive
To build a better town...

And that's why the
People won't give up
And the people
Won't give it a rest...

The people won't give up
Until they passed every test!

Success!
Just give it a rest,
Because they're
Building you up
Just to tear you down…

They're building you up
Just to set fire to your town!

And the people didn't
Give a damn…
And the people won't
Give it a rest…
Because you've got to
Try and survive

So try to pass this test!

DOWNHILL

If there's a chance
It doesn't seem correct,
And maybe a chance
I might have been
Giving folks heck,
Then try to understand
By and by...
Try to never recommend
Living, giving, on the sly...
Because it's like driving
At breakneck speed...
When in a world so selfish,
And seeing nothing but greed,
Life seems hellish-

What's a world without relics
Of a nation reborn...
Of your brightest shining hour
When your shame was shown...

Trust as you know
Is the story that is told
Betrayal is only for the weak
And truth for the bold...

The strong will survive,
As only the righteous can tell...
The strong will survive,
As they eat to live well!

That's the world we live in
Straight is the road
And narrow is the path
To a world renown!

Those were the days
When TV shows made sense
Those were the days
When it wasn't past tense...

Never learning
Never growing
The evil deeds men do
Headed to reaping what
They are always sowing...
Because one day our lives
Won't be so blue!

Downhill it's gone
And not original...
It's gone forever
And sure is pitiful!

Going downhill
Searching for a cheap thrill
Passing the buck
While the preachers today
Are down on their luck

On the heavenly train
On our way to a better world
On the heavenly train
Giving your dress a twirl!

You must learn to leave
Your cares behind,
And let your worries be few...
Take caution to the wind,
In a world so perfect and
So brand new!

THE RAREST FOLK

The rarest folk
For a different stroke
As we walk to the
Beat of a different
Drum-beat-drum...
We haven't got long,
A brassy-sassy song,
Even if you're out of tune
Or drunk and high strung!

Life you're given...
Hard knock life you're living...
Sweet Georgia Brown
And the world loves
A winner now!

Sassy song
Say it all night long...
The smell of time,
By the bell and the rhyme!

The rarest folk
For a different stroke
And a little heaven-on-earth drug
For a little sweep under the rug...
To the beat of a different
Drum-beat-drum!
In the bottomless pit of love
He gonna see it gets done!

Get you some knowledge
For the rarest folk
Get you some knowledge
It takes a different stroke!

For the rarest folk
And the drama queen...
For the rarest folk!

Because the drama is
Still mean!

THE ANSWER

I arrived at the question
So what's the answer?
Where all the nations
Are unsure...
And all sins still like a cancer

When all else fails
Let love prevail and be
Like the only cure...

When all else fails
You have to always be sure...

At the start of a whole
New beginning
As we reap what is sown
Out of good...
Only then are we winning
With a brand new start
In the neighborhood!

If you arrive at the question
You'll get the answer
You'll have it all for yourself,
If only you take a chancer!

If you're not for-realing
In your life,
Then you are fake...
This world is in such disarray
That it distorts your vision
In a negative way...

So try to be stronger
You'll last a whole lot longer..
It's the only answer
So now just take a chancer!

THE HIGH AND THE MIGHTY

The high and the mighty
Got your back
The high and the might
Must always be on the attack!
For a little heaven-on-earth drug…
For a little sweep under the rug…
For a little heaven-on-earth drug
In the bottomless pit of love…

The high and the mighty
Rivers so deep…
The high and the might
Rivers do wide…
Face the honest truth
Face it just like Ruth…
Die together!
Wearing silks, satin or leather…
No matter going north
Steady headed south
If you're not singing in tune…
Then just shut your mouth!
Change while living east,
And be blessed in the west
Or delusions for illusions that
Are tricks of the mind
At their very best!

THE ENDS THE MEANS

This race
This world
This gangster pace
Has always been
Where it's at
Right where it's supposed be...
In a world that never was flat...

Until...
The end comes surely,
Until...
The end comes silently,
Until...
The end comes swiftly,
Until...
The world ends defiantly...

The ends
The means
The Amozula
Who wins

Let love live!

The ends
The means
The Amozula
Who wins?

Let love live!

A flower
A choice
The rose
The song

Millions standing strong!
Millions singing all the
Day long!

Your hopes, dreams, and
The power...
Your hopes, dreams and
The trying hour!

THE GOOD SONG

It was the perfect ending
To a marvelous beginning
It was the baddest song
You've never heard
Anything so strong!

And makes love last
The whole night long…
Then you're only winning…
Let love and the living
Make earth spin on and onnn….

Can't get it out of my head
It's only good
Because you'll never be misled…

It's the good song
That keeps you rocking
All day long…It's the good song,
Makes you feel you can
Last all the night strong!

Until all hearts have bled
Love lasts and is strong…
Least and least said
It's the good song!

So use it,
Never abuse it,

Just love it,
And rise above it...

So use it,
Never abuse it,
Just love it all your
Life long...

Because that is the
Only perfection
From something so strong!

MEET AND GREET

And if you're down for it
You'll love it!
Meet and greet
I'm a part of it
I'm above it!
Meet and greet
Makes life so sweet
And you've got the
Upper hand…
Folks will learn something
They all can understand!
Here I am
I'm here at last!
Here I am
Death is a part
Of the past!
Meet and greet something great
Meet and greet something
So grand….
Meet something so sweeter
Than the legends
Of the motherland!
Meet and greet
The One with the master plan…
Meet and greet
In the Amozula land!
Meet and greet
During this great endeavor…
Meet and greet the finer ones

No matter what the weather!
Meet and greet
The One with the
Master plan..
Meet and greet
In a world so grand!

IT'S CLEAR

It's only clear to me and them...
That your understanding
Is at the level of ten!
Falling apart and washed away...
Gotcha sold in your mind
While the waters rage!
It's clear you are seeing
Things that aren't there..
It's clear your are believing
That you lost your hair!
It's clear you can't read
The words on the page...
Hands off the drama queen
While she's on the stage
Visions of sugar plums
Putting you in a trance
Visions of sugar plums,
Making you wanna dance!
It's clear there is confusion
On your part
It's the only thing coming
Straight from your heart...
It's clear to me
That now your understanding
Is the level of number three...
So listen and read the only
Good book...
Listen and read
You're only a dumb crook...

Because trouble is the only
Thing you're gonna see...
You'll reap what you sow
Out of your own misery!
Start using your head...
Everything sacred and good
Won't be last
Won't be the least...
Or totally dead...

SOMEBODY'S SWEET FOOL

The joy

The privilege

The loner

The liar...

And the sweet music
Has the base in your face
While lifting you up
A little bit higher!

Somebody's sweet fool...
Makes you wanna
Break them golden rules...

Got an angel on my shoulder
Give me the strength to
Walk proud and be
A lot more bolder...

Putting you in range
While taking you higher...
Making you feel something strange
So just put out the fire!

Somebody's sweet fool...
Needs to go back to school...

Quit trying to pretend
That a bad habit
Is your bestest friend!

Can you stand in the rain
While breaking them golden rules again...
Can you try to pass the test...
Until you find yourself
A total mess!

The joy
The privilege
The loner
The liar...

Because the music
Has the bass in your face
While lifting you up
A little bit higher!

A RARE THING

It's a rare thing
Sit this one out
And don't be watching me dream!
Because those are the most
Precious ones…
So hear the drum beat-drum
And I'll sing you a happy song

Pray for a better fate
Because heaven has
Decided to wait!
Hanging your hopes
On a world so brand new
A rare thing
A precious dream
Now matter how tough
Or difficult
Life may seem!

I AM HERE

Here I am
I'm here at last!
Will finally be free
Death-
Will be a thing of the
Past!
We'll leave this tired
Old world-
Don't wanna stay...
Here I am-
I am here...
Eternity is so very,
Very near...
Eternal life to live,
Not separation-
Got to let-love-live!
You're my everything,
You're my world...
You're my everything...
And as precious as silk,
Diamonds and pearls!
Here I am-
I'm here at last!
Here I am- Death is a thing of the past!

FALSEHOODS

Your love for falsehoods is
Your story-book ending
Your love for the drama
Qualifies a means to an ending

Got to sit down and brainstorm
Keep your focus
Like the way bees swarm
Born a more perfect creation!

With ideas that are bold
And sold throughout this
Entire nation!

Falsehoods not the reality
That you're making it

Falsehoods not the be-all, end-all
Of what you know that's
Totally at stake in taking it!

Falsehoods for all the pain
Falsehoods for all the pleasure
Falsehoods won't get you in
God's good graces…
With each sinner seeking to endeavor!

Falsehoods putting you in the groove…
Falsehoods for all the world

To try to improve!

So get lost
Or get-to-stepping!
Falsehoods gotta go…
Or I'll get a weapon!

Falsehoods for a story-book-ending
Falsehoods for who likes to be pretending
Reach some more
For what others think is to high

Falsehoods forever wondering
And asking the question why!

Your love for falsehoods is
Your story-book-ending!
Your love for the drama
Qualifies a means to an ending!

THE AGONY THE EBONY

A red rose can never die
For a gangsta-thankstah
Giving you sanctuary on the sly

The Agony The Ebony
What our lives used to be

The Agony The Ebony
So many more golden memories!

A flickering flame that never dies
It can be a song of love
That whispers in your ear
The question-Why!

The Agony The Ebony
What are lives used to be

The Agony The Ebony
So footloose and fancy-free!

A red rose can never die
For a gangsta-thankstah
Giving you sanctuary on the sly!
The Agony The Ebony
Is all that I need

The Agony The Ebony
For the better things in life

You're using to succeed

The Agony The Ebony
Reads: My life's sensation...

The Agony The Ebony
Leaving my heart to bleed
All over this nation!
And say hello to the richest
Memories of our past
So when you are finally
In understanding
You're totally free at last!
The Agony The Ebony
My peoples story...
The Agony The Ebony
To God be our glory!

THE EXPLOITATION

Because the contradiction is
A joyous affair
Can't you see?
That you were made
Totally aware...

Because the joy of
A hope in a better world
Is not a joke...

We must continue to do
Right- Survive
Arrive!
If you want to receive
That promise and new
Hope!

There it is
There it was

Saying your goodbyes
Going going gone for good
And this is all because!

I turned this daredevil task
Into a monumental affair

So now if you're ready
To close your eyes
And shut your ears

You better get on to it

So now if you are ready
To shut your eyes
And close your ears

It will be a deafening sound-
So just go ahead and do it!

So get ready
To rise above it

So get ready
To rise above it!

To see something
Like no other

Just rise above it!

KEEPERS OF THE LEGEND

Keepers of the legend
Keepers of the dream
Keep climbing higher peaks
And swimming through streams

The legend
The lover
The river
The stream

Walking with the host
Spending time with
The ones you love the most

Bitcher…richer!
Moving down the
Mountains fast
Throwing a stone
At a house made of
Glass…

Keepers of the legend
Are freed at last!

The legend
The lover
The river
The stream

Ain't nothing like
Those golden memories
Got to always treasure them
For as impossible as it
May seem

Become ten times richer!
And ten times bitcher!
Moving downhill fast...
And you are having a blast!
Throw a stone at a house
Made of glass
Keepers of the legend
Are freed at last!!

DEADLY STORM

It's gi-normous!
The tornado is the
Storm hanging over us
Reaking havoc
And causing destruction
Reaking havoc
Where there was no introduction!
Play sweet elevator music
To drown out your sorrows
Playing sweet elevator music
Just can't be beat the drums
To drown out a million
Bad tomorrows!
You can't see through me
To the river and the well
Until it runs dry
You can't see it to well…

The deadly storm
It's gi-normous!
The tornado is the storm
Hanging over us
And closing in fact
So when we're no longer
Suffering…
Then we are free at last!

DIVIDED UNDECIDED

We're divided
Always undecided
Whereas we were once
Together ...
Birds of a feather
One big happy family
United
One big happy family
Never undecided

Knowing your history
You'll always be alright
With it!

Stayed strong completing it
Stayed strong and destined
To be repeating it
In your ears
Until it's your only sad song
In your ears
Because it will make you
Strong!

Divided and always alert
Decided and always
Putting in the work
Yes it was all for you!
Yes until our work
Is finally through

Then we'll run the course
To walk hand in hand
All the way to the blessed
Promise land!

Divided undecided
It's the real thing
Divided undecided
You must be righteous
And real...

Will you be there
Or will you be square...
Don't know just be you
It's something that's fair
Face the honest truth
Don't know just be you
It's the bitter pill
You got to be true!

Divided and showing
You all the signs
Decided that our
Love is real
With no more designs!

Which do you choose?
How much can you stand
To lose,
Is it only a matter of time...
Which do you choose
How much can you stand to lose
For a tale left further behind!

For a little heaven-on-earth
Drug as we all know it
For a better world
Where the good stay young
God only knows it!

This will be the escapade
The big picture
This will be the escapade
Cast on you from God's
Good graces!
Poor or richer!
So now who is the wiser?
If it gets more ugly
More undecided...
Ten times richer!
If it gets more ugly
More undivided
Even if it makes me
Ten times bitcher!

I once thought it was my misery
Was blind but now I see

Divided-
As many hearts I break
I'll mend...
Decided-
To try and do the right thing

So if tomorrow be the
Great day...
Then the horns will sound
And the bells will ring
So let's start to play...

Music, we all can use...
Walking in your own steps
On a bigger brighter day
You just can't lose!

Divided Undecided,
Let's do the right thing...
For a little heaven-on-earth
Drug....
Divided Undecided
In the bottomless-gottomless
Pit of earth'slove
Let's do the night thing!

IT'S HEREDITARY

In you the righteous brotherhood
Where God in heaven made
Everything great and good...
Are one in the Amozulas
To be made one with the Amozillas

Making your voices loud and proud
Where the amazons are rich
And the Sheikhs where the shroud

It's legendary!
Because when it's gold you
Can hit it...
If it's legendary
You can find it in a go-see
And you can say you did it!

If it's ancient, try to match
Wits with it...
In you he makes everything
So great and good
That it comes to be a perfect fit!

In you the amozula
Raised and made one in the
Motherland...
It's carried from sea to shining sea
So that it can be made to be
A thing so grand!

In you the righteous brotherhood
Where God in heaven made
Everything so great and good...
Leads us to a bright new beginning
Because when we strive for perfection
We will always be winning!

AMOZEKE! AMAZON! AMOZULA!

Amozeke! Amazon! Amozula!
when no one else can...
Is the mother of all mothers of
a foreign land!

When I was sick, they nursed me...
when I got well, they rehearsed me...
when all hope seemed lost...
here's the legend of your

Amazeke! Amazon! Amozula!
in the place of no winter frost!

Amozeke! Amazon! Amozula!
Quite legendary!

Amozeke! Amazon! Amozula!
Quite Extraordinary!

Amozeke! Amazon! Amozula!
So the whole world can see...

Amozeke! Amazon! Amozula!
How much you Amo-mean to me!

Amozeke! Amazon! Amozula!
From river to river...

Amozeke! Amazon! Amozula!

No different form one, or the other!

The A in Amozeke... wider than the river!
The M in Amazon...for the love the motherland has given her!

The O in Amozeke...to keep us going strong!

The Z in Amazon...because you'll never forget this song!

The U in Amozula...wider than the river!

The E in Amozeke...
IN YOU THE AMOZULA!

Amozeke! Amazon! Amozula!

Restore the race...

Amozeke! Amazon! Amozula!

Back to our ancestors place!

Amozeke! Amazon! Amozula!

Restore our riches...

Amozeke! Amazon! Amozula!

Put the thieves in ditches!

Amozeke! Amazon! Amozula!

Make the crooked places straight!

Amozeke! Amazon! Amozula!

Give the dry places rain for the flowers to mate!

Amozeke! Amazon! Amozula!

Land of Kings and !Queens!

Amozeke! Amazon! Amozula!

Will never see an end to their reign!

Amozeke! Amazon! Amozula!

Because seeing is believing...

Amozeke! Amazon! Amozula!

That your hope in them is Amozeke-receiving!

Amozeke! Amazon! Amozula!

Will always make a way...

Amozeke! Amazon! Amozula!

So that no one takes away!

Amozeke! Amazon! Amozula!

A peoples so strong and proud...

Amozeke! Amazon! Amozula!

A rich heritage so sing it out loud!

Amozeke! Amazon! Amozula!

I'm so proud to announce...

Amozeke! Amazon! Amuzula!

Is such an invincible force!

Amozeke! Amazon! Amozula!

Take from thieves hands...

Amozeke! Amazon! Amozula!

And restore back to the mother land!

Like the Z in Amozula!
Back the motherland!

Will Amozeke-receive you from
evils hand!

Amo-sing it out loud and wear it proud!
From one place on earth to the other...

LIKE NO AMO-OTHER!!!

Amozeke! Amazon! Amozula!

I love amo-yula!

Like no amo-other!
Like no amo-other!

Amozeke! Amazon! Amozula!
when no one else can...
Is the mother of all mothers
of a foreign land...

When I was sick, they nursed me...

When I got well, they rehearsed me...

Amozeke! Amazon! Amozula!

When all hope seemed lost...

Amozeke! Amazon! Amozula!

In the land of no winter frost!

Amozeke! Amazon! Amozula!

No ordinary...

Amozeke! Amazon! Amozula!

Quite extra-ordinary!

Amozeke! Amazon! Amozula!

So the whole world can see!

Amozeke! Amazon! Amozula!

How much you Amo-mean to me!

Amozeke! Amazon! Amozula!

From river to river!

Amozeke! Amazon! Amozula!

For the love the motherland has given her!

Amozeke! Amazon! Amozula!

Wider than the purest ocean!

Amozeke! Amazon! Amozula!

Is more than just a notion!

Amozeke! Amazon! Amozula!

Makes waves over the ocean!

Amozeke! Amazon! Amozula!

Is more than just a notion!

Amozeke! Amazon! Amozula!

So the whole world can see!

Amozeke! Amazon! Amozula!

How much you Amo-mean to me!

The A in Amozeke
Wider than the river!

The M in Amazon
For the love the motherland
has given her!

The O in Amozula
To keep us going strong...

The Z in Amozeke
Because you'll never forget this song!

The U in Amozula
Wider than the river...

The E in Amozeke
For the love the motherland has
given her!
To keep us going strong...
IN YOU THE AMOZULA!!!

Amozeke! Amazon! AmoAfricans!
searched high and low all over the lands!

Like the A in Afri-can
LIke the M in Muzonta
Like the O in Osei
Like the Z in Zutundra
Like the E in Effect
Like the K in Kurekh!

Like the E in Effect

And the K in Kurekh

Mountain so high!
Valley so low!

Mountain so high!
To the river it flows!

Mountain so high!
Valley so low!

Mountain so high!
To the river it flows!

Like the A in Amozeke!
Like the M in Moshesh!
Like the A in Amozeke!
Like the Z in Mozique!
Like the O in Zutondra!
Like the N in Otunba!

Like the O in Zutondra...
And the N in Otunba!

Live on in Amazon and reign eternal-zon!

Live on in Amazon and reign eternal-zon!

Live on in Amazon....

and reign eternal-zon!

Live on in Amazon...
and reign eternal-zon!

Like NO! Amo-Other!
Like NO! Amo-Other!

AMOZEKE AMAZON AMOZULA PART 2

Amozeke Amazon Amozula
when no one else can...
Not one, not two, but three
Is the mother of all
Mothers of a foreign land!

Not one but two...
All things become brand new
It's the renown
After all devils reap what they
Have sown,

Sooooo.....
Keep up the pace!
Amozeke Amazon Amozula
Will keep on running this evening
Race!

Like the Z in Amazon
Because you'll never forget this song
Like the U in Amozula
Because in you I'll always feel
So strong!

The L in the love
They have given me

The A in Amazon
From river to river
Sea to shining sea!

Amozeke Amazon Amozula
Will restore our riches back to our
Ancestor's place...
Let devils reap what they have sown
From our majestic motherland space!

Amozeke Amazon Amozula
Land of kings and queens
Amozeke Amazon Amozula
Will never be an end to their reign!

So see it!
Feel it!
Dream it if you can
Don't hinder the mother of all
Mothers of a foreign land!

Because success is glorious!

Catch the feeling
Catch the vibe
Catch the spirit
And amozeke-arrive!

The power is yours
To open all closed doors!

Amozeke Amazon Amozula
Won't lead those too scared to follow
Amozeke Amazon Amozula
Won't lead me into temptations

Sacred and hollow!

Amozeke Amazon Amozula
Will take back what is ours
Out of evils hand...
Amozeke Amazon Amozula
Will restore it back to the motherland!

Amozeke
Out of evils hand
Amazon
Back to the motherland
Amozula
From ancient times
Across the desert sands!

The race-
Put all devils in their place
That time
So beautiful and so fine!

Amozeke Amazon Amozula
Old things are brand new...
Amozeke Amazon Amozula
Not one- but three- not two!

The mother of all mothers of a
Foreign land
Pray that God will keep them
In his hands!

And the greatest gift was
Handed down...
To all in the african land
Making and doing good

So safe and so sound!

The truest word
The truest gift
The truest word
Is putting me into rhythm!

So where the trouble begins
Lusaka ends...
The mother of all mothers
Of a foreign land to our
Family and friends!

So sing!
Dance!
And celebrate once old
Is brand new...

Amozeke Amazon Amozula
Will take you to a better place
With skies so blue!
Like no amo-other!
Love your enemies
Love your brother
Old-
But amozeke-receiving
Everything which is new!

In you the amozula
A more perfect creation
To witness a gift that will
Rock the enitre African nation!

And pick you up
Just to turn you around
Just to witness this truth
So that you can be kingdom bound!

Yes!
It will always be good
For the shu-in...
Amozeke Amazon Amozula
Making you feel so brand new again!

MADE ONE

Made one to be whole...
Receive this knowledge
Because it's good for your soul!
And you knew the trio
Was here to stay...
To show their great powers
On that righteous day!

If you can just start to believe it...
Straight hair is when you
Receive it!

Where all life on the earth began...
In the mother of all mothers
Of a foreign land!

When I was sick
They nursed me
When I got well
They rehearsed me...

Amozeke Amazon Amozula
When all hope seemed to be gone
Amozeke Amazon Amozula
Here is the legend of the three
Giving you a brand new song!

Amozeke Amazon Amozula
Quite legendary

Amozeke Amazon Amozula
Quite extra-ordinary!

Amozeke Amazon Amozula
So that the whole world can see

Amozeke Amazon Amozula
How much they will always
amo-mean to me!

AMOZEKE AMAZON AMOZULA PART 3

Amozeke Amazon Amozula is not done...
Amozeke Amazon Amozula with the power
That has only just begun!

Amozeke Amazon Amozula I feel alive again...
Amozeke Amazon Amozula has arrived to
The world with a bigger plan!

Amozeke Amazon Amozula
To make the evil cease...
That tries to stop our motherlands inner
Peace!

Here to restore our riches back
To the land...
More wealth numerous as the desert sands!

Here is the legend of the three
Breaking off the chains
And solving all the worlds mysteries!

Mysteries no one could answer
Come together, be bold and
Take a chancer!

Not just a song
It's the greatest story

Ever heard and hoped for
The gods grace, goodness and eternal glory!

Amozeke Amazon Amozula
Because seeing is believing...
Amozeke Amazon Amozula
That your hope in them is
Amozeke-receiving!

Will put the thieves in ditches
Will return to the motherland
All of her riches!

Granting all your wishes
And making you feel great...
With joy and hope
In love there's no hate!

Amozeke Amazon Amozula...
I love amo-yula!

So let's keep on running at this pace...
So that we can arrive at the key answer
For this political race!

AMOZEKE AMAZON AMOZULA PART 4

In you the amozula
Making you cry tears of joy...
Can be amozeke-receiving
All of her rewards-
Whether the strategy used is
For real or can be considered a ploy
So here's the deal...

Rise above!
Come together all African nations
Rise above!
To regain the worlds richest sensations!

If you-
Amozeke Amazon Amozula-
Is always believing...
If you-
Amozeke Amazon Amozula...
That your hope in them is
Amozeke-receiving!

Because the gift of being...
Is always going to be
Amozeke-receiving
All the way back to the motherland...
You of the african race regaining
All the rewards taken back out of

Evils hand!

Let's come together as a people
Let's come together as a tribe...
To count the miracles
To count the moments
Do goodness and amozeke-strive!

Amozeke Amazon Amozula
Is a family who is a tribe...
Going back, back, way back
To when that ancient sun gave
You that special vibe!
Amozeke Amazon Amozula
Of the african race...
Will keep on amozeke-surviving,
And keep up this generational pace...

Amozeke-prove as you amozeke-move
Across the african continent...
Amozeke-prove as you amozeke-move
You are still gonna be wanting it!

Because one day the evil will cease,
And all good things given back to
Our ancestor's as we strive to maintain
The Amazeke Amazon Amozula's
Eternal peace!

Change!
And bring about change...
Come as you are or just
Stay the same...
Change!
And bring about change...

Rainbows emerging after the rain!

Through all kinds of weather
And for a better tomorrow...
Ceasing all pain
And ending all your sorrows!

Dance sing and shout...
Run where ever those feet can go...
So that the inhabitants can witness
A great, entertaining show!

So let our stories be bold...
Be true, righteous, legendary
And never sold!

The charm, the chance-
Change gonna come soon...
The charm, the chance-
Let the sun shine forth...
And the night skies reveal the new moon!
Give it to the gods to be a winner...
Go boldly forth as you have
In the beginning!
And strengthen the African nation
To make her surpreme...
As the land is filled joy, hope,
And the motherland with precious things!

Yours tossed in the wind like a windmill
Can't you see?
Yours tossed in the wind like a windmill
Amozeke, Amazon, Amazula
Means so much to me!

Amozeke, Amazon, Amozula
Will be the new world left to reason...
In every bit of happiness joy...
And singing praises for this new
Amo-season!

Like no amo-other-
And learning to love your brother...
As we are singing in tune...
The song of the earth,
The song of the moon!

The wisdom you see,
The knowledge you know...
So that we all can reign in triumph
And you can both learn and grow!

THE LEGACY OF THE SULTAN

Moultan the Sultan has got them in a snare
Amozeke, Amazon, Amozula has always
Got to be aware...
Of the crammed monkeys to the Sultan's queen
At the feast of the Nile who will always
Cling to one heart and one dream!

And as they chase out the evil from the
Valley of the Nile who all speak one language
On the camels they are perched on in which
They ride...

Across the desert sands...
Giving hope to all the foreign lands!
Building their hopes and reaching goals so high...
They you could not count the desert sands
Sweet by and by!

Amozeke, Amazon, Amozula has got the
Sultan in a snare together they band...
Amozeke, Amazon, Amozula has the upper hand
And by their knowledge their powers are diverse
Where there's a need they will fulfill it
For all common good from earth to the universe!

The strength in you is with higher designs,
The meaning of their name is truth...
Possessing the power for all times!

So if you listen...
To the sounds of the drummer man
Telling the story of an ancient land
Yet in his hands lie fate!
Better hear how they slow down fast
At his master's command:

Mon-Khessan!
No average man!
Where the trouble begins...
Lusaka ends!

AMAZE AND AMAZON

Making miracles all over
This African nation
Amaze and Amazon
Rewards sensation!
Boatless, coatless, shipped
To shores...
Hopeless, boatless,
Speak no more!
Amaze and Amazon will
Sing everyone a beautiful song
Like a rose planted by a stream...
To follow a path to the
Impossible dream!

Sing-a-ling,
Sing-a-long...
Because it's your favorite
Place to be...
Sing-a-ling,
Sing-a-long...
Making history!
So remember this story
And not to sell your soul...
For ancient dust
And ancient gold!

THE SENSATION OF AMAZE AND AMAZON

Hand in hand...
Two steps forward,
Hand in hand
Fight for the things
You hope for more of...
And after the rain
I hope you see the sun...
That will come shining forth
Soon your work is done!

And pick you up,
Just to turn you around...
Respect for mankind...
Amaze and Amazon!
Strength is their power
Fighting for all your rights
For the mother of all
Mothers of a foreign land...
And to end all impoverished
Plights!

To make miracles all over
The African nation...
The drums the rewards
Will always be your sensation!

Giving shelter
Giving strength
To all who are wise...
Giving shelter
Giving strength
The drums-
The reward
Is watching the sun rise!

The surest, purest conquest
You ever seen before...
Amaze and Amazon
Will bring back the legends
And give you the rewards!
Sing dance celebrate
Look to the sky
Never forget the past
And learn from it...
You can if you try!
Because even when
You know your history
Your strength is your song
Never forget this lesson
Amaze and Amazon!

Remember these heroes
Goodness the only way
Remember these heroes
Will help you to overcome
Tribulations every day!

Amaze and Amazon,
The legends of ancient times...
Amaze and Amazon,
Defeated all evil and

Conquered to master
The rhyme!

A perfect world
A perfect friend...
Is the mother of all
Mothers of a foreign land
Not a fable but a perfect blend...

Of legends in time,
Of legends in stories...
Ringing in each new year
With ancient dust ...
And this ancient golden glory!

AMOZEKE AMAZON LONG GONE

So take one another by the hand
Because in you the Amozula
Will truly love, protect,
And understand
Remember the first and savor
The last...
Remember the traces in
Your past!

Long gone, so far away...
Long gone, that Amozeke Amazon
Amozula might be here to stay!

So take one foot and put it
In front of the other
Take this hope in them
And renew your mind
For the love of the mother
Of all mothers of a foreign land!

Decide in your mind the amount
Of knowledge so you may
Understand...
And carry this message
From river to river
So that the whole world can see
How life came from within her!

The song is long,
The song is strong...
For the Amozeke Amazon long gone!
It's making those has-been like
No amo-other...
From river to river
From daughter to mother!

Like nothing so less than
Anything so fine...
Like nothing so less
Than the magic of a casual design!
A trio so renown
It can never be a disgrace
A trio so renown
That it turned the motherland
Into a sacred place!

The mother of all mothers
Of a foreign land so old
It's all brand new-
The mother of all mothers
Of a foreign land
So old and renown
That it could be the hope
Where the help is only for you!

Come home to the motherland
So you can experience the mysteries...
Come home to the motherland
So you can be a part if her
Histories!

Nothing in this world compares
To something so grand!
Three heroes one vision
Of the mother of all mothers
Of a foreign land!

QUALITIES OF THE Z-KINGS

Qualities!
Sureness!
Desire ...
In its pureness!
You can't go so low
But only yet so high...
Gonna run this race
And put out this fire!
While searching
Higher heights
And climbing
Deeper depths
The revelations
Is its sureness
The revelation
Was the reality
At it's purest!

Qualities
Sureness
Desire
It's pureness
You can't go no
Lower but yet
So high...
Got to run this race
While searching
Higher heights!
Got to run this race
So what's your desire?

THE REVELATION OF GREATNESS

Because the revelation
Is greatness
Because together you
Can't feel any more
Forsaken
And the revelation
Made them whole
For God had cause
To make all devils
Reap what they
Have sown!

Yes together!
Tight and smooth
Like leather…
We'll weather the
Storm
Yes together
Tight and smooth
Like leather
You knew this
All along!

Yes it was
All for you
The most righteous
Eternal wisdom
Is the most realest
Of God's greatest

Truth!
So seek to endeavor
Seeking the truth
To face this moral
Wisdom like honest Ruth!

SONG OF THE Z-KINGS

Because the kings are alive
Because the kings are rich
The kings are alive
There's no contradiction
It's-
Going to go without a hitch
It's-
Singing you a happy song
So you can feel the bliss

To the glory
To the legend
To the triumphant

And to the strong
Yours the lucky number
Seven to string you right along

To the glory
To the legend
To the triumphant

In heavens hallowed halls
Yours the lucky number seven
Making good the glory
Of the law!

Because the kings are alive
Because the kings are rich

The kings are going to thrive
No misses, no hits!
A heritage so proud
You could go on singing
This song...
A heritage so profound
You could never ever
Feel the contradictions!

So feel the joy, feel the love,
Of the mother of all mothers
Of a foreign land coming
From up above!
So read the story, feel the truth,
And face this moral compass
So that you won't feel the blues...

No more contradictions
No more hesitations
Feel all of the rich history
Throughout the African nation

With song with strong
You could feel the sensation...
With song with strong
Convictions for in you
The revelation!

Ingram Content Group UK Ltd.
Milton Keynes UK
UKHW040006280323
419070UK00008B/27